The Andersons

Jim

Nell

Helen

The Whitmans

Kat

Mr Whitman

# My Best Friend

# AND THE ROYAL RIVALS

Mary, Queen of Scots

Queen Elizabeth I

Sally
Morgan

Illustrated by
Gareth
Conway

To my darlings, Daisy and Lily.
Being a princess sounds terrible!

Published in the UK by Scholastic Children's Books, 2021
Euston House, 24 Eversholt Street, London, NW1 1DB
A division of Scholastic Limited

London ~ New York ~ Toronto ~ Sydney ~ Auckland
Mexico City ~ New Delhi ~ Hong Kong

SCHOLASTIC and associated logos are trademarks and/or
registered trademarks of Scholastic Inc.

Text © Sally Morgan, 2021
Illustrations © Gareth Conway, 2021

ISBN 978 1407 19579 7

Printed and bound in the UK by CPI Group (UK) Ltd, Croydon, CR0 4YY

2 4 6 8 10 9 7 5 3 1

Papers used by Scholastic Children's Books are made from wood grown in
sustainable forests.

www.scholastic.co.uk

Dear Reader,

You have in your hands a collection of **TOP-SECRET** letters.
These letters have criss-crossed the English countryside, survived
murderous plots and evaded the snooping eyes of **ROYAL SPIES**.
They've been sewn into smocks, buried in heaps of dirty laundry
and concealed in a sheep's stomach (sorry if they are a bit smelly).

These letters hold important information about one of
history's most infamous royal rivalries. On one side, there is
Queen Elizabeth I of England, a powerful Protestant queen unlike
any the world has ever seen, and on the other, Mary, Queen of
Scots, a Catholic queen in exile, removed from her throne and
imprisoned in England for almost twenty years.

Both queens had royal blood, both had a claim to the throne of
England, and both had supporters willing to lay down their lives in
their honour, but neither queen was safe while the other lived.

Kat worked in the court of Queen Elizabeth I. We met in
London in 1584, just as I was about to leave my aunt's house to
live and work with my mother as a laundress for Mary, Queen of
Scots. These are the letters we wrote to one another as we tried
to make sense of what we saw going on around us, desperate to
understand how two cousins – with so much in common – could
become sworn enemies.

I hope you enjoy reading our letters.

Love,
Nell

8th October 1584
Wingfield Manor, Derbyshire

Dear Kat,

How are you? I am so happy to have met you. To think if you hadn't got into that 'spot' of bother (get it?) with your father's ruff[1], we may never have met.

## THE STORY OF OUR FRIENDSHIP SO FAR!

Did you manage to get the ruff dry in time for your father's performance? I know ruffs can be an awful fiddle. How did you get the

1. A fancy frill made from lace or fine cotton worn around the neck.

ink on it in the first place? Were you writing to someone? I don't know many people who can read or write,[2] so I can't tell you how **HAPPY** I am to have a pen pal.

I promised I would write, didn't I? I am so sorry that my first letter is to say **GOODBYE**. I am not in London any more. I hoped so much to see you again under less **URGENT LAUNDRY BUSINESS**, but alas even more **URGENT LAUNDRY BUSINESS** has called me north.

My mother works as a laundress for Mary, Queen of Scots, who is living at Her Majesty Queen Elizabeth's pleasure here in Wingfield.[3] Mother has worked for Mary's household since she was a girl. My father worked there, too, in the cellars seeing to the barrels of beer[4], but he and many others were let go when Queen Elizabeth decided Mary did not need so many people to work for her. This all happened when I was little. Father took me with him to London to live with my aunt and my cousins. I liked living with my cousins, but I missed my mother a lot, so I was **THRILLED** when Mother sent word that a nearby brewer had a job for Father and I could work with her.

I am very excited. I will be working for a **REAL QUEEN** at a **REAL CASTLE**. I know she is a **QUEEN IN EXILE** and doesn't rule a country and I know that the castle is sort of a **PRISON** and she isn't allowed to leave, but I am excited nonetheless! I wonder what Mary is like?

In London, I heard all kinds of stories about her. Some said she was

2. At the end of the sixteenth century, only about one third of men, and one in ten women, were able to read and write. These men and women were usually very rich but some poorer people, like Nell, did know how to read.

3. After being forced to give up her throne and being imprisoned in Scotland, Mary, Queen of Scots, escaped in 1567 and fled to England. In England she hoped her cousin, Queen Elizabeth, would help her raise an army to take back her throne. Instead, Queen Elizabeth held her prisoner and kept her under close watch.

4. This would have been a busy job as most people at this time, including children, drank beer instead of water, as the water available was often too dirty to drink. The average person drank almost five litres a day.

**BEAUTIFUL** and **GLAMOROUS** and could charm the birds from the trees. Other stories described her as being a **HERETIC⁵ MONSTER**, determined to **KILL QUEEN ELIZABETH** and take the throne for herself. I asked Father, but he said I could decide for myself soon enough. I promise to tell you **EVERYTHING** that happens.

It took my father and I more than five days to get here. We walked all the way, finding shelter in barns and sheds as we travelled. One kind family let us stay with them for a night. My feet were sore, and it was lovely to eat some warm soup rather than **STALE BREAD**. I had to sleep **NEXT TO A COW**, but I didn't mind. She slept soundly and didn't move too much. My father was with the hens. He **DID NOT** look well rested the next morning.

5. A heretic is someone who holds beliefs that are different to what the majority of people believe. Mary, Queen of Scots, was called a heretic because she was a Catholic and England and Scotland were Protestant at the time. Many Catholics, including the pope, believed that it was actually Queen Elizabeth who was a heretic.

6. In the sixteenth century, very wealthy people slept on mattresses stuffed with animal hair and feathers; less wealthy people slept on beds of straw, often alongside their animals.

When we arrived at the village, Mother was there to meet me and I was so happy to see her. I can't believe I am going to **SEE HER EVERY DAY** and work with her.

Wingfield isn't what I was expecting at all. I'm not sure if I thought Mary would be cooped up in a cell, but Wingfield is far from a horrid prison. Mother says Mary is allowed out and about, and can even receive visitors. She sends lots of letters and has her own staff, including cooks, secretaries, dressmakers and ladies' maids. She has her own **HORSES** and even a groom who takes care of them. I'm not sure many prisoners could boast of that. She is even allowed to ride out to go hawking.[8] Admittedly her guardian, Ralph Sadler, as well as forty or more **ARMED GUARDS**, accompanied her on horseback, but she was out in the world nonetheless.

Will you write back? Please say that you will! I know so few people who can write and fewer still with anything interesting to say. I can only write because my uncle taught me my letters. He works for a printer; so I know a lot about how to get ink stains out of clothes! I told Father that I wanted to write to you, and he said he might be able to help. He used to work as a post rider, riding up and down the country with letters and parcels for people. He gave it up a long time ago, but he still knows some of the riders. I hope this gets to you!

You said your father was a musician at the court of Queen Elizabeth. That must be exciting. Do you live at court? Does your mother work there too?

Do write back if you can!

Yours,
Nell

---

7. Hawking is a type of hunting that uses specially trained birds of prey such as hawks, falcons and even eagles to catch small birds and mammals.

10th November 1584
Court of Queen Elizabeth, London

Dear Nell,

I can't believe you have gone! Of course, I will write to you. You will be my **FRIEND IN EXILE**. That sounds rather exciting, doesn't it? Much more exciting than a pen pal. Not that I have many of those. I was so excited when the rider found me! It made me feel important. I think he was surprised to be bringing a letter to a lowly musician's daughter.

Yes, my father is a musician and has served the queen since before I was born. He has played music since he was a boy and was taught the trumpet by his father who came to England with the court of King Philip of Spain. We do live at court, which can be exciting but is also very busy. As well as the trumpet, Father can play the lute and sings wonderfully. He has taught me to play too; though I don't have quite enough breath to play the trumpet, I can pick out a tune on the lute. I love to listen to him play with the court musicians. There are about thirty of them. He gets to wear fancy clothes, which are bought for him by the queen, and plays whenever the queen requires music – which is **ALL THE TIME.**

Zzz...

Queen Elizabeth likes to have music at dinner, music to be played as she walks in and out of rooms and she even likes to have music playing first thing in the morning so that she can have a dance before breakfast. It's a lot. Father and the other musicians work hard to learn the latest tunes and practise old favourites to keep her entertained. As well as all the performances, Elizabeth's court often moves around between the royal palaces, and every time we move, I have to help pack everything up. It is **EXHAUSTING.**

I like to listen to Father play, but I like to hear him sing the most. There's a special song he sings for me that he says Mother used to sing before I was born. My mother died giving birth[8] to me so this song means A LOT. The song is about blessings and Father always says that he feels blessed that I wasn't taken, too.[9] He says Mother loved music as much as he did and was **MUCH BETTER** at playing the lute than he was. I wish I could have heard her play. I can't imagine how happy you are to be working alongside your mother. I hope you cherish her.

I like to sing and play music like Father, but girls aren't allowed to become musicians, no matter how well they play and he says that it's even harder for people who look like us. Father always reminds me that we have to work **TEN** times as hard and be **TEN** times as good as everyone else in the room.

8. Giving birth in Elizabethan times was much more dangerous than it is today. It is estimated that the mother died in two out of every hundred births at this time.

9. This was considered a blessing because childhood was also much more dangerous in the 1500s. Out of every ten children born, only seven would be expected to live to their tenth birthday. Without modern medicine or vaccines, diseases killed many more children than today.

That's why he made sure I learned how to write.

I also help maintain the uniforms of all the musicians, which keeps me VERY busy. I don't mind though. I love all the fine cloth they wear. Musicians get to wear **MUCH FANCIER CLOTHES** than other people of their status, because they represent Queen Elizabeth. All of their uniforms belong to her, which is why I was so upset about the ruff. I didn't want to get Father in trouble. I'm so glad you **SWOOPED** in and **SAVED THE DAY!**

One day, I would like to be able to make clothes like the musicians' uniforms, as well as gowns for the ladies at court. Father is saving up money so that I can become an apprentice to a draper.[10] In the meantime, I learn what I can from the ladies of the queen's household.

I have not met Queen Elizabeth, but I have seen her many times. I like to hide on the balcony with the musicians to watch the dancing at court. She is a **FABULOUS** dancer and I can tell she enjoys it a lot. Father says she is a good musician, too.

The queen certainly has a lot of admirers. The court is filled with gentlemen telling her how **BEAUTIFUL** she is and swearing they are **SICK WITH LOVE** for her, but I think she is more spectacular than beautiful. She is a bit like the sun, in that you can't seem to look directly at her because she is so dazzling. Her gowns are covered in gold thread and jewels and her ruff is made of the finest white lace. Her face is **VERY** white too[11] and her hair is a rich red. No other lady at

---

10. To get into certain trades, parents had to pay for their children to be taken on as an apprentice. As an apprentice, the child would live with the tradesperson and work for them for little to no pay until they had picked up enough skills to be able to go into business for themselves.

court can compare to her.[12]

I was so set on getting the ruff clean when we met, that I didn't explain to you how it came to be in such a state. Father had asked me to bring it to him for the night's performance, but on the way I met a young man named Samuel Grant. Sam stopped me and asked if I knew where I could find the queen's principal secretary (otherwise known as the **ROYAL SPYMASTER**), Sir Francis Walsingham, as he had come to court to work for him. I told Sam I had no idea where Walsingham might be. He blushed at this and said he had heard Walsingham had dark skin and had presumed he was my father! Can you imagine?

11. Queen Elizabeth wore thick white make-up made from lead and vinegar to cover up scars left by smallpox.

12. They didn't dare! Queen Elizabeth struck the Countess of Leicester's ears when she arrived at court in a dress the queen thought was too extravagant.

I told him Walsingham got his nickname, 'the Moor'[13], because he **WEARS BLACK** all the time, not because of the colour of his skin.[14] Gosh, I'd hate to be Walsingham's daughter. I've seen

13. 'Moor' in the sixteenth century referred to a person of North African origin.

14. Queen Elizabeth I loved to give people silly nicknames, and because she was the queen she could pretty much call people anything she wanted whether they liked it or not. Rude!

him sneaking around court, looking suspicious of everyone. I can't imagine he'd be much fun at all. Even if that wasn't the case, how silly to assume two people are related just because they have a similar skin tone! I pointed this out to Sam and he was extremely embarrassed and admitted that it was ignorant of him to think such a thing.

I asked him why he was looking for Walsingham anyway and he said he hoped to travel the world as one of Walsingham's spies. He knows how to speak lots of languages[15] and he said he had also been teaching himself 'ciphers'.

When I told him that I didn't know what a cipher was, he almost squealed with excitement. He took out some parchment and a quill he had in his trunk and, right there on the stairs, wrote out the alphabet. He said a cipher was a way of writing in secret code so that other people couldn't read what was written. He drew out a different shape under each letter and said some codes were just letters out of place but that we could use symbols instead of letters. I even learned how to **WRITE MY NAME** using the cipher! It was tricky at first, but I could see how it might work.

Sam's excited to work with Walsingham and is hoping to become one of his best cryptographers,[16] deciphering important messages and uncovering secret plots.

He said it was important work because the safety of everybody in the country rested on uncovering plots against

15. Walsingham was said to speak French, Spanish, Latin, Greek and Italian.

16. A cryptographer is an expert in ciphers and decoding messages.

the queen, of which there have been many. He said he couldn't wait to sign something called 'The Bond of Association'.[17] He said it was an important pledge to protect the queen. It gave a small group of people the power to act against anyone found plotting against Queen Elizabeth and anyone who would benefit from such a plot, even if they **KNEW NOTHING** about it. I asked what 'ACT' meant and he said, '**KILL!**'. I told him I couldn't imagine him being capable of killing anyone, and he stuttered and said he would mostly be in charge of office work and not really involved with the **POINTY END** of things.

Its name is Bond. The Bond of Association, Bond. It's a licence to kill.

BOND OF ASSOCIATION

I did say that a good spy would have known that I was not Walsingham's daughter and perhaps wouldn't have given up this much information during our very first encounter.

17. The Bond of Association was drawn up by William Cecil and Francis Walsingham following a plot against the queen's life. The Bond stated if a plot against the queen's life was discovered, anyone in line to inherit the throne would be banned from doing so and executed, even if they were unaware of the plot. The Bond was sent all over the country and signed by everyone loyal to Queen Elizabeth, including Mary, Queen of Scots.

He seemed offended at this and said he wasn't actually a spy just yet, which I assured him was a good point.

Then we returned to writing secret messages using the cipher. I was so focused that I didn't notice when **A RAT** scurried over my foot. I **SHRIEKED** and jumped, knocking over the inkpot and splattering it on the ruff which lay nearby. Hence, the stain. Sam tried to help but he was already late for his meeting with Walsingham. Besides, I wasn't entirely sure he wouldn't make things **WORSE**. I ran off after that, which is when I bumped into you (**SORRY!**). I hope I see Sam again though. I would like to know more about ciphering and being a spy.

I am sad that you have gone, though I am glad to have a pen pal in exile. Do you think you will ever come back and work with your uncle? Does he still work with the printer? It must be fascinating. Though perhaps not as interesting as serving **A CAPTIVE QUEEN**. Do tell me all about her! I can't imagine a queen being locked up. Is she really **A MONSTER**? I wonder what she does all day… Without a country to run and with people there to do everything for her, I imagine she must get rather bored.

Yours gratefully,
Kat

P.S. This is my name in cipher. I have attached a page of the cipher in case you want to try and write in it too.

# TOP-SECRET CIPHER

A B C D E F

/ ⊓ o Υ c 4s

G H I* K L M

o- ∞ τ ℅ ℑ ~

N O P Q R S

3 ℥ n ∈ S #

T V* W X Y Z

α - ℓ ℓ ℮ ℒ z

*Notice anything odd? In the Elizabethan alphabet the letters 'i' and 'j' were the same, as were 'u' and 'v'.

15

Dear Kat,

Goodness, cipher looks so **CONFUSING**. I had a hard enough time learning to read and write when the letters were in the proper order; I can't imagine ever being able to make head nor tail of a message written in cipher. You and Sam must be very clever indeed.

How exciting to become an apprentice to a dressmaker! Queen Elizabeth sounds breathtaking. I would love to get the chance to be **DAZZLED** by her one day. I would love even more to get the chance to wear one of her gowns. I was hoping that as laundress to Mary, Queen of Scots, I would be able get up close to all of her wonderful gowns. She has lovely ones made by her own dressmakers from fine silk sent by friends and relatives in France and Italy.[18]

Instead, I wash sheets, smocks, stockings and handkerchiefs. Mother says this is because washing gowns, which are mostly made of silk and cloth of gold,[19] would ruin them. Such a shame. Still, I do hope I get to wear a gown like that one day, even if just for a moment. I suppose you'd be able wear them all the time if you made them yourself!

I like working with Mother though, and I promise I do try to cherish her, even when she nags me. I missed her terribly when I was

18. These deliveries of cloth and accessories are thought to have contained hidden messages from Catholic relatives abroad.

19. 'Cloth of gold' was fabric woven from silk thread wrapped in a fine strip of real gold.

living with my uncle. I hope I return to London to see him one day. Printing is so interesting, they publish all sorts of pamphlets and books, which are worth a fortune.[20] He only works as an assistant, but he would let me in the shop sometimes if I promised to behave. I always wanted to play with all the little letters that were put in the press, but he said they were too valuable.

Mary, Queen of Scots, is **NOT A MONSTER** at all. She is generous to her staff - often giving them gifts - and she loves animals, especially **DOGS**. She has quite a few of them and talks to them all the time! My favourite is a fluffy, white dog named Hamish. I try to save him scraps from my dinner and play with him whenever I can.

Mary doesn't have to spend any time governing as she doesn't have a country to govern, and she only travels when Queen Elizabeth wishes to move her to a new secure location. From what I have seen, she spends most of her time doing embroidery and talking to her ladies, some of whom have been with her since she was small. The ladies sit on low stools around the queen who sits on a **MAGNIFICENT RED VELVET CHAIR**, which is hung with a fine lace Cloth of State.[21]

The queen is **BRILLIANT** at needlework. She has made some beautiful pieces. My favourite is one of an orange cat that wears a crown and has a mouse by its paw. It looks so lifelike. I told Mother about it and she said it sounded like a 'cat that got the queen'.

20. The printing press was still a relatively new invention in Elizabethan times. Pages were set with moveable type and printed individually. Although printed books were expensive, they were much cheaper than the handwritten manuscripts, which meant more people in England could read them and ideas could be shared more easily.

21. 'Cloth of State' is a rich cloth that usually hangs behind a throne to form a backdrop.

Who knows what that means? It would be so much easier if people could just say what they meant.

Mary sends an awful lot of letters to her family and friends, but Mother says the secretaries probably write most of those. As much as I **LOVE** sending letters to you, it must be nice having someone else do all the writing.

I wouldn't necessarily call Mary **PRETTY**, but have heard that she was very **BEAUTIFUL** and **CHARMING** when she was younger. She is tall, and Mother said she used to love to dance and hosted extravagant balls. I find that hard to imagine now. She mostly looks sad and annoyed these days, as I am sure I would after being imprisoned for all this time. She is also ill a lot. Mother said that is due to the damp air and feeling so unhappy all the time, but there are rumours the queen might be faking it.[22]

Do you think Elizabeth is in as much danger as people say she is? From your description, her court sounds like it is one long party. Is it really like that? Do tell me more. I can't imagine I would want to dance all the time if I knew people were out to kill me.

I do hope this letter gets to you!

Yours,
Nell


P.S. Here is a sketch of Her Majesty's needlework of a cat. Can you see what Mother means by 'cat that got the queen'?

22. It's true. The queen was known to put on an illness to get sympathy from people. She used every method she could to get people to pay attention to her.

30th December 1584
Richmond Palace, London

Dear Nell,

Thank you for your letter. It gave me such comfort hearing from you. Be assured, Queen Elizabeth is in **TERRIBLE DANGER**. I have seen it for myself! We are in Richmond, which is not so far outside of London. The queen likes it here because of the beautiful park and the gardens. I like them too, though I try to stay out of Her Majesty's way. I was exploring these gardens when I saw a man attempt to **KILL QUEEN ELIZABETH**.

I'd just finished my chores and was taking a walk in the garden when I saw that the queen had come out to enjoy some fresh air too. I ducked behind a hedge until she walked by. As I waited, I spotted a man hiding behind the hedge in front of me. He waited until the queen walked past him before he stepped out from behind the bush and drew **A DAGGER** from his sleeve. I tried to shout but I was **FROZEN IN FEAR**.

Thankfully, it seemed, so was he! His arm was raised, ready to **MURDER** the queen, but instead of bringing the dagger down and ending her royal life, it stayed where it was. His face was one I will never forget. It was fixed with an expression of **PURE TERROR** as if **HE** was the one in danger. I suppose in a way he was, for within a moment the queen's guards were at her side, and the man and his dagger were hauled away!

Father had told me that there were **LOTS** of people that wanted to see Queen Elizabeth dead, but I had not believed it until I saw it with my own eyes. Who could want to see the end of such a gentle and noble queen?

When I told Father about the horrible ordeal afterwards, he said that the man would be tried and executed in a most awful manner. I remarked that surely all manners of execution were awful and he said, 'while you are right, the punishment for

23. A man named William Parry attempted to assassinate Elizabeth I in the gardens of Richmond Palace towards the end of 1584. He claimed he was unable to complete the task because he was so dazzled by her royal presence and her resemblance to her father King Henry VIII that he froze. This was one of many attempts on the life of Queen Elizabeth I.

treason is much crueller than any other.'[24]

The queen doesn't appear to be frightened at all. If I thought there were assassins lurking behind every corner I would never go out unless I really had to, and if I did, I would be surrounded by armed guards. Instead, Queen Elizabeth travels from palace to palace, greeting crowds as she goes. Father says that this drives her advisors crazy, but that she believes as an 'anointed queen' she is protected by God. I asked if he believed it. He said that the **MOST IMPORTANT** thing he had learned since moving to England was that it was safest to believe whatever the person sitting on the throne thought you should.[25] But he did think a few more men with swords here and there might help, too. Ha!

Everyone is saying that the assassin's name is William Parry and that he was put up to it by Mary, Queen of Scots. Do you think that could be true? People at court do love to gossip. Let me tell you a bit more about them!

There's the queen obviously, but I have told you all about her. She is always marvellously dressed, as are her ladies-in-waiting who are usually dressed in a way to make her stand out.

Then there are Queen Elizabeth's advisors. One of these is Walsingham, who I mentioned in my last letter. He is always dressed in black and **NEVER SMILES**. I think he might be the **GRUMPIEST** looking man I have ever seen. From what

---

24. The Elizabethans were very creative with their punishments. They used burning, hanging, beheading, boiling in oil, public starvation and cutting off limbs to make an example of those who committed crimes and to deter others thinking of doing the same.

25. In England, people were not allowed to worship as they wished but had to follow the faith of the king or queen. Not doing so could mean punishment and even death. This was the same for many countries in Europe at this time.

I've heard, he doesn't like your mistress, Mary, at all. Or any Catholics, for that matter.

Then there is Lord Burghley, William Cecil, who is the secretary of state and the queen's chief advisor. It's his job to know how much money the queen has, where it is coming from and where it goes. He's also in charge of something called the 'Privy Council' which always makes me laugh. Get it, privy?![26] Imagine having your own toilet council!

Now, Your Majesty, the council and I would recommend at least two wipes for that. Can I get you a fine lambs' wool cloth? Or would you like me to call the first lady of the bedchamber?[27]

26. Privy comes from the French word *privé*, which means private. Going to the toilet is also something that is considered private, which is why toilets were called privies for centuries.

27. The first lady of the bedchamber was in charge of helping the queen with going to the toilet, which no doubt was a bit of a job in such an enormous dress.

The Privy Council is actually a group of men[28] whose job it is to advise the queen on what to do. (Nothing to do with toilets at all!) Of course, she gets the final say on everything, but they give her the information she needs to be able to make those decisions.

As well as the Privy Council, the queen is usually surrounded by her ladies-in-waiting. The most important of these is a woman called Blanche Parry, who has looked after the queen since she was a baby. She is with the queen nearly all the time and must know **EVERYTHING** that is going on in the realm. I have heard when people have fallen out with the queen or need a favour from her, they go to Blanche for help.

Now, now, my lady, you must eat your peas!

The queen also has a lot of much younger ladies-in-waiting whose job it is to keep her company and do anything she might need doing. Otherwise, there aren't many other ladies at court. The queen doesn't seem to like it, so all of her advisors and courtiers are instructed to leave their wives at home.

28. Yes, they were all men. Ugh.

I suppose if I was the queen I would like to be the centre of attention too. And she certainly is that. Everyone at court acts like they are totally and utterly in love with her.[29] The person who seems most in love with her is a man named Robert Dudley, the Earl of Leicester. The queen seems to rather like him too, but Father says they have been like this for years and aren't likely to marry. In fact, the only two men who do not seem to be IN **LOVE** with the queen are Walsingham and Lord Burghley, who look miserable because they are so worried about her, and after the assassiation attempt I saw, I am not surprised.

How are you settling in to Mary's court?

Yours,
Kat

P.S. Hah! I like the picture of the needlework. I think it's more code! The ginger cat in the crown is Queen Elizabeth and Mary is the mouse! Just like the cipher. Mary sounds very clever.

---

29. This is true. Men at court were advised to leave their wives at their home in the countryside. Many wrote very romantic letters to the queen and even wrote songs and poems about how much they were in love with her.

Dear Kat,

How frightening! You must have been terrified to be so close to an assassin. I am glad the queen wasn't hurt. I am not surprised Lord Burghley and Walsingham are worried about her safety, but I don't see how Mary could be responsible, cooped up so far away. Besides, she and everyone else in the household has been too busy.

No sooner had Father and I arrived at Wingfield that we had to move **AGAIN** - so much for settling in! Moving a queen is no mean feat. Everything Mary owns and all her staff had to be packed up and carried **MORE THAN TWENTY MILES** south of Richmond Palace to Tutbury Castle! The queen rode by herself, surrounded by more than forty armed guards on horseback. The armed guards weren't to protect Mary, but to make sure **SHE DIDN'T ESCAPE**! And the household followed behind with horses and carts piled high with all of her furniture, tapestries, countless gowns, jewels and everything else she owns, which I am sure you can imagine is **A LOT**.

I asked one of the servants, a girl named Agnes, why we had to move and she said it was because Queen Elizabeth had heard about Mary's hawking excursions and visitors and wasn't **PLEASED**. And so the man who was in charge of Mary has now been relieved of his duties. He has known Her Majesty since she was a baby and couldn't help being so kind to her.

Mary has been given a new jailor, a man named Amyas Paulet. I have not met him yet, but from the sounds of his rules he is **DREADFUL**.

# THE CRUEL RULES OF SIR AMYAS PAULET

• Mary, Queen of Scots, may have **NO** visitors.

• All letters addressed to and from Mary, Queen of Scots, must be read and copies passed on to London.

• Mary, Queen of Scots, may not ride out hawking and will only be allowed out when **ABSOLUTELY NECESSARY,** under the guard of soldiers armed with muskets.[30]

• Mary, Queen of Scots, may not distribute alms[31] to the poor.

• Laundresses are to be **SEARCHED** before and after taking laundry to the village.

I'm not sure what is meant by 'searched', but no decent man could insist on searching beneath our smocks, surely? I asked Mother and she laughed and said she'd like to see him try, as she **THWACKED** a pile of wet linens with a hefty swipe of her battledore.[32]

30. An early form of shotgun.

31. It was a tradition for rich people to give purses filled with small amounts of money to poor people they met when they went out. Sir Amyas was probably worried Mary would attempt to pass messages in this way.

32. A battledore was a wooden bat used for beating laundry when it was wet in order to force the dirt out of the weave. Items similar to this battledore have been found dating back as far as ancient Egypt!

I hope not, battledore or no battledore, as that is how I am planning on getting this letter to you!

I do not like Tutbury **ONE BIT**. Mother says Mary has lived at Tutbury before and hates the castle. I can see why. It is **DAMP** and **HORRIBLE**.[33] With the forced move and the new strict rules, she must be even more unhappy.

Mother and I and the other laundresses don't live in the castle itself, but in a cottage in the grounds. I have to enter the castle every day to pick up the laundry. I don't like going in there at all. I always feel like I am being watched.

That's why I don't see how Mary could have been involved in sending the assassin. Nor can I see why she would - when it would put her in so much danger. Not only is she aware of the Bond of Association, she signed it herself! Mary knows that, as next in line to the throne, she would face her share of 'cruel and unusual' punishment if a plot was discovered.

I can't help but think that, if Queen Elizabeth would visit Mary, if they could sit and **TALK** with one another like they each do with their ladies, they might actually be **FRIENDS**. But instead there is all this talk of plots and murder. It all seems rather **SILLY** to me. Did you know they have **NEVER EVEN MET**? Why do you think it is so important that Mary is kept prisoner and watched so closely?

I wish there was a way they could both live in peace with one another.

Your friend,
Nell

---

33. Tutbury was known to be draughty and smelly, too!

8th February 1585

Court of Queen Elizabeth, London

Dear Nell,

I did know they haven't met. It's unbelievable, isn't it? You would think they had, they are cousins after all! And they have so much in common, too. They are both queens. They both love animals and love to dance and are both well educated. In fact, they have far more in common than you and I yet they seem to spend so much time being suspicious of one another.

Perhaps it runs in the family. Did you know, Queen Elizabeth was imprisoned by her OWN sister, Queen Mary I of England? Queen Mary I suspected Elizabeth of plotting against her when she was on the throne. She ordered Elizabeth to be sent to the Tower of London. Isn't that **HORRIBLE**? Elizabeth must have been terrified, especially after what happened to her mother.[34] No one was able to find any proof of a plot and they made up before Mary died, but that is **NO WAY** to treat your sister if you ask me.

I asked Sam why Mary, Queen of Scots, is considered such a risk and he said it's because she's a Catholic and because some think she has a claim to the English throne. He said there were battles throughout much of Europe about whether countries follow the Protestant or Catholic faith and that many people have lost their lives in these struggles.

34. Elizabeth's mother was King Henry VIII's second wife, Anne Boleyn. Anne Boleyn was beheaded at the Tower of London on 19th May 1536.

Walsingham, and many of the queen's most trusted advisors, fear that something like what happened in France in 1572, the Massacre of St Bartholomew, could happen here if Elizabeth does not keep a tight grasp on the throne and keep England a Protestant country. During the Massacre of St Bartholomew, a violent mob of Catholics swept through Paris, murdering French Protestants. Walsingham's pregnant wife and child fled just in time, but he had to stay back and witnessed it all. Sam said their work was important to stop the same from happening in England.

So, they intercept Mary's letters and keep her under watch to prevent rich Catholics from Europe — many of whom are her relations — from contacting her and sending an army to rescue her and take the throne.

Some say Queen Elizabeth has been tolerant towards Catholics up to now, but her sister Queen Mary I was less tolerant of Protestants. Queen Mary I put so many Protestants to death during her reign she was nicknamed **BLOODY MARY**.[35] They say she caused chaos by outlawing Protestant mass, and returning England to the Catholic faith. People fear if Mary, Queen of Scots, or indeed any Catholic came to the throne, he or she would be a **BLOODY MARY II**.[36]

I heard there may be some good news, though. There may be a way for Queen Elizabeth and Mary, Queen of Scots, to

35. More than 300 Protestants were burned for heresy in just three months during Mary I reign.

36. In fact, Mary I was not as 'bloody' as people say. Her father, Henry VIII, put many more people to death during his reign and caused far more chaos when he changed the country from the Catholic to the Protestant faith and placed himself as head of the church. Though not as bloody as her father, Elizabeth I is thought to have called for the execution of AT LEAST as many of her subjects for heresy as her sister.

live in harmony with one another, if not in the same country.
I heard Lord Burghley say that Queen Elizabeth wants Mary
to return to Scotland. She has written to Mary's son, King
James VI, to ask him to welcome his mother home and share
his throne with her. Don't you think that would be a wonderful
solution? Not only will it reunite a mother with her son, but
also Mary would be **FREE** and **QUEEN** of a country again.
Also, King James is a Protestant and **LOYAL** to Elizabeth.
He will keep an eye on his mother and make sure she is not
plotting anything. Not that I think Mary would plot against
her own son. If this works out, do you think you would have to
move to Scotland, too? I don't think I would like that. Scotland
is even further away than you are now and so our letters
would probably take **EVEN LONGER**.

Do you think your mistress would accept such an offer?


Your hopeful friend,
Kat

20th March 1585
Tutbury Castle, Staffordshire

Dear Kat,

Thank you for your letter. It filled me with **SUCH HOPE**. It would have been wonderful if James would agree to share the Scottish throne with his mother. Not only would she be able to rule again, but she would also be reunited with her son, who she has not seen since he was a baby.

Alas, there will be no such reunion. I dropped a pile of clean linens in the mucky courtyard yesterday (yet **MORE** stains!) as I was startled by the awful wail coming from Mary's rooms. I feared she may have injured herself, but I found out later she had received a letter from King James. The letter said that he will not allow her to return to Scotland for fear her return will cause his Protestant subjects to rebel against him. Protestant nobles in Scotland drove Mary out the first time so they have no desire to see her return.[37]

Alas!

If only she could get them into the laundry basket

The queen is beside herself with grief. Mother and I are readying ourselves for a hamper full of handkerchiefs. I only wish there was more I could do.

Imagine having the power to free your mother from prison and **DOING NOTHING**. Or having the chance to meet a mother you never got the chance to know, who is desperate to be with you, and **TURNING HER AWAY**. I'm not sure I will ever understand how a family can treat each other in this way. So much plotting, so much suspicion. Can you imagine them all sitting around the table together? You'd have to hide the knives, that's for sure.

I hope King James's refusal to take Mary out of England doesn't push your mistress to do something drastic. It doesn't seem possible that such a sad and lonely woman could be responsible for something as terrible as a massacre, nor can I believe that she could put someone to death, never mind hundreds. She has many Protestant servants and treats us all kindly. Agnes says she is generous and often gives her maids gifts, and she is so kind to her pets too. I can't believe this gentle woman is as much of a menace as Sam says she is.

Your not-so-hopeful friend,
Nell

37. Scotland's Protestant nobles did not want to be ruled by a Catholic queen. They worked against Mary from the moment she arrived in Scotland from France in 1561. They did everything they could to undermine her authority and eventually imprisoned her and took custody of her son. Mary escaped to England in 1568, where she looked to her cousin Queen Elizabeth for help. Instead, Elizabeth imprisoned Mary and kept her under close watch for nearly twenty years.

15th April 1585
Court of Queen Elizabeth, London

Dear Nell,

It must have been dreadful for your mistress to receive such a letter from her only son. I wish more than anything that my mother could be here with Father and me. I would give **ANYTHING** to have had the chance to get to know her.

King James didn't get the chance to know his mother either, but when given the opportunity he turns it down! Can it be that he is such a terrible son? Or is Mary so terrible that even **HER OWN SON** doesn't want to know her?

I will admit, your description of Mary is very different to how many here describe her. I am not sure what to think; can she possibly be both a pitiable figure, as well as a threat to the security of the nation?

Maybe King James is doing what a good king should do, and putting the needs and safety of his country first? I don't know. One thing I do know is that I would not want to be king or queen of a country, or even **THE WORLD**, if it meant not seeing Father again or causing him harm in any way.

I hope the queen receives some happier news soon.

Yours truly,
Kat

10th May 1585
Tutbury Castle, Staffordshire

Dear Kat,

No happy news here, unfortunately. Far from it. The queen's new jailor, Amyas Paulet, has arrived. He is the man responsible for the horrible new rules and what do you know, **I DO NOT LIKE HIM ONE BIT**. He has thin red hair with a pointed nose and beady eyes, and he is **ALWAYS SNOOPING**. He seems permanently suspicious and takes a peculiar delight in being mean and horrible. I think he would be better suited in charge of a prison for common criminals than of a queen. I understand she is a queen in exile, but she is still a queen.

Until now, Mary has been able to run her household as though it were a royal court and as though we are all her subjects. Of course, there have been limits, but she has been kept as comfortable as possible and treated as a queen.

Mary's chair, though not quite a throne, is covered in red velvet and woven with the finest cloth of gold. Above her chair hangs a **'CLOTH OF STATE'**. Mary's Cloth of State is finely embroidered with the words 'En ma Fin gît mon Commencement' ('in my end is my beginning').

Sir Amyas believes that a Cloth of State is for kings and queens only, and that Mary is not a queen. To him there is but one queen in England and that is Queen Elizabeth. Whenever he goes into Mary's rooms, which he does often and unannounced, he **TEARS DOWN** her Cloth of State.

Not only that, but he does not listen to her either, not in the way one is supposed to listen to a queen. I once saw him turn his back on her and walk out of the room while she was still speaking!

Can you imagine anyone behaving in such a way to Queen Elizabeth? It must make Mary, Queen of Scots, furious to see how low she has fallen that a man such as Sir Amyas Paulet can be allowed to treat her in such a way without being punished.

It is hard to imagine how the situation could be worse for her.

Yours truly,
Nell

Dear Nell,

Amyas Paulet sounds just like Walsingham! How horrible for Mary to be treated that way. I can't imagine anyone turning their back on Queen Elizabeth. I **DREAD TO THINK** what would happen to a person who did such a thing![38]

I heard someone at court say that Queen Elizabeth had made the right choice in Paulet as jailor for Mary. They said he is a strict Protestant who is more loyal to Her Majesty than anyone they have ever met! He is said to be sharp too and that **NOTHING** will get past him.

You will be careful, won't you? I love receiving your letters, but I would hate for you to do anything that would make him angry or get you in trouble.

Sam says, with Paulet in charge, they will be watching Mary's every move, especially after her own son turned his back on her. This was her only hope, her son. Sam said that Mary must be desperate and is sure to slip up sometime soon, and Walsingham and his men are ready to catch her the moment she does.

Your friend,
Kat

---

38. Queen Elizabeth was known to 'box the ears' of subjects who upset or insulted her, which means she would hit them hard around the head. She would also banish them from court and never speak to them again.

Dear Kat,

I will be careful. I promise. I almost got myself into the most **TERRIBLE TROUBLE**, but it wasn't for writing letters. I don't know what I was thinking! Do you remember me saying how much I wanted to try on one of Her Majesty's gowns? Just to see what it was like? Well, I did something very silly.

I was on my way to collect the queen's bed linen, as it wasn't with the laundry when we were about to start the wash. I don't often get to enter Her Majesty's chamber, and when I did, it was empty. I saw a gown. It was a **RICH, FOREST GREEN** and embroidered with cloth of gold, and it was just **ABANDONED ON THE FLOOR.** I couldn't resist taking a closer look.

At first, I thought I would only touch it. But I got carried away and next thing I knew, I was wearing Mary's gown. Made of beautiful velvet, it was thick and soft and really, **REALLY HEAVY**. The gown was **MUCH TOO LONG**[39] for me but I didn't care. I was trying - and failing - to twirl in it (again, it was **VERY HEAVY**) when I heard a noise behind me. It was one of Mary's maids, Agnes, and my mother. I thought I was going to faint, when my mother bustled in apologizing and assuring Agnes that I would be punished within an **INCH OF MY LIFE** before dragging me down the steps.

---

39. Not surprising. Mary, Queen of Scots, was said to have been six feet tall!

Mother was **FURIOUS!** She said I was trying to lose not only my job, but hers, too. She asked me what I would have done if I had **TORN** the gown. I could have ended up in the stocks or prison or **EVEN WORSE.** She said I was lucky that the maid would have been in almost as much trouble for leaving the dress on the floor as I was for trying it on.

As punishment Mother has me collecting up all the chamber lye for the wash and then treading it into the linens. Chamber lye doesn't sound so bad, does it? I love how grown-ups give things fancy names when they mean something yucky. Chamber lye, though, is **PEE**.[40] I have to go around the household collecting it from the chamber pots in a sloshing bucket. Once I have enough, I pour it into a big tub called a bucking tub. The smell is terrible. I try not to breathe but that only makes it worse because when I do, I take such a huge gulp of air it feels as though I am swallowing it.

After I have poured the pee into the tub, I put in the linens and then remove my shoes and stockings to climb in after it. I tread in the lye for hours. Mother says this is the best way to remove stains and to get the queen's laundry really clean. Usually she gets one of the younger girls to do it, or Mabel because she has **LOST** her sense of smell. Ugh! It is disgusting! I'm not sure my feet will ever smell like themselves again! But it could have been **MUCH** worse. I won't even **THINK** about putting on the queen's gown ever again.

Later, when I saw Agnes, she beckoned me over. She begged me not to tell that she had left the queen's gown abandoned on the floor like that. She had been called away urgently

Wee must learn to behave ourselves.

40. Chamber lye is gross, but pee contains ammonia which is very good at getting out stains.

and hadn't managed to hang it up properly. I promised I would keep her secret as long as she kept mine and told her how Mother was **PUNISHING ME**. She wrinkled her nose and said she was glad she got to work with the gowns instead of the linens. She's in charge of brushing them down with a clothes brush and makes any repairs before putting them away. I told her how I would love to be able to sew and do fine needlework and she said she would teach me.

I'm **SO** excited. I'm not sure where I will find the time to learn to sew. You'd be amazed how much laundry a royal household makes. That and having to collect all the chamber pots. I hope Mother doesn't have me doing that for much longer. I don't want to **LOSE MY SENSE OF SMELL** like poor Mabel.

Your foul-smelling friend,
Nell

30th July 1585
Court of Queen Elizabeth, London

Dear Nell,

I think I can smell your feet from here! How awful! I can't imagine having to tread the lye. That sounds **ROYALLY DISGUSTING**. Pardon the pun. Ugh! I had no idea someone had to do that, but I don't suppose I'd ever really thought about it.

You really must be careful. As terrible as your punishment is, imagine what would have happened if someone other than Agnes or your mother had found you? Imagine if it had been Paulet ... or even Mary, Queen of Scots, herself!

I am pleased about you learning to sew with Agnes. Needlework is much less smelly than laundry by the sounds of things. If you get good enough, perhaps you could do that instead.

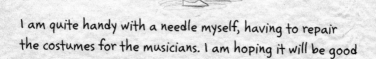

I am quite handy with a needle myself, having to repair the costumes for the musicians. I am hoping it will be good training for when I become an apprentice. Wouldn't it be wonderful if we went into business together? If we made dresses we'd be able to try them on whenever we liked. We could wear velvet and silk and cloth of gold. Of course, we couldn't wear them out,[41] but it would be magical to see one another dressed up like fine ladies, don't you think?

Your friend,
Kat

P.S. If linens are washed in pee, why don't people's clothes smell terrible?

---

41. Laws known as the Statutes of Apparel meant that only people of high social status, who were very wealthy, could wear the finest clothes. These laws meant people could see who was influential in society just by looking at someone, but they were rarely enforced. Fabric such as silk and wool from overseas was reserved for only the highest social status people, with purple silk for royalty only. Kat and Nell would have worn rough linen and wool from England.

20th August 1585
Tutbury Castle, Staffordshire

Dear Kat,

You asked an excellent question! Laundry is a **MURKY WORLD FILLED WITH SECRETS**. We are rather like magicians with the power to make stains (and odours) disappear. Like magicians, we must never reveal our tricks or we go against a sacred code, passed down from mother to daughter for generations. If I told you, I would have no choice but to **KILL YOU**.

Hah! Just kidding. The trick to getting rid of the smell is, after the linens have been in the lye, you have to rinse them really well in fresh water. That gets rid of most of it. Then we leave them to dry in the sunniest spot we can find. The sun makes the linens whiter and drying outdoors gets rid of any leftover smell. As an extra trick, we spread linens over scented herb plants such as rosemary or lavender. Once we are done you would never know about the chamber lye or the stinking bucking tub. Clever, eh? If only I could do the same with my feet.

I love your idea of going into business together! Though I am not sure I will be much help with the sewing. My first sessions with Agnes have been rather bloody affairs. I seem to want to put the needle into my fingers more than I do the fabric. I like to sit with Agnes though; she tells me all sorts of things about Mary and about life in Scotland before Mary fled.

Did you know Mary, Queen of Scots, tried to **ESCAPE FROM PRISON DRESSED AS A LAUNDRESS**? Apparently, the boatman realized she wasn't one because of her soft, white hands. Ha! That would be a dead giveaway. My hands are red from scrubbing the clothes and being in water all day, and now my fingertips are covered in needle pricks, too!

washerwoman and
clumsy sewer

definitely not a washerwoman
(perhaps a queen?)

## OTHER IMPORTANT FACTS I LEARNED ABOUT MARY, QUEEN OF SCOTS

• Mary has been **MARRIED THREE TIMES!** Once to the heir to the throne of France, who died soon after becoming king

• The second time was to a man named Lord Darnley; he was James's (now King of Scotland) father. Darnley was **MURDERED!**

• After this a man named Lord Bothwell **KIDNAPPED** the queen. Lord Bothwell was one of the conspirators thought to have murdered Darnley, and for some reason Mary married him!

Can you believe that last bit? Agnes says some in Scotland believed that Mary marrying Bothwell was proof that Mary was in on his plan to murder Darnley. They think she had wanted Darnley dead because he was a terrible husband. Agnes doesn't believe that. She says that Bothwell forced Mary to marry him, and that he was a horrible bully and an even worse husband than Darnley.

The Scottish lords did believe it though; they said they had letters to prove it, too. They separated Mary from her son, forced her to give up the throne and put her in prison. Agnes says she doesn't believe in these letters and think it was an excuse to get Mary, a Catholic, off the throne.

After all the drama - being married three times, widowed twice, kidnapped by husband number two's murderer and then marrying said kidnapper - you'd think Mary would appreciate the peace and quiet of imprisonment!

I mentioned this to Agnes but she **DID NOT** find it funny! She said the queen is miserable. She has rheumatism[42] in her legs that makes them swollen and she finds it hard to walk. She says that being in prison makes the queen unhappy, too. I guess it isn't really very funny, when you think about it.

When Agnes and I sit together to sew, Hamish often sits with us. Agnes says it's because I give him bits of bread I save from my dinner, but I like to think it's because he **LIKES ME FOR ME AND NOT THE BREAD.** I know he belongs to the queen, but I like to think he's my friend too.

Can you believe Mary has been married three times? Do you think Queen Elizabeth will ever marry?

Your bloody-fingered friend,
Nell

---

42. A disease which causes joints in the body to swell and become very painful.

25th September 1585
Court of Queen Elizabeth, London

Dear Nell,

Hamish sounds **SIMPLY ADORABLE**. Mary must be lonely.
I'm sure it's comforting that she has such a wonderful
companion. Queen Elizabeth is quite fond of animals too.
She has many dogs and even a ferret.

I had heard Mary has been married three times. None of
her marriages went particularly well for her. It doesn't seem
like she had very good taste in husbands. Not that queens
usually get much of a choice in the matter.

I don't think Elizabeth will ever marry, though she
isn't short of suitors. Her father was the worst husband in
history![43] While Elizabeth remains unmarried she is in control
of the country and of what she
can do. If she were
to marry, this power
would transfer to
her husband.
I sure wouldn't
want to give
all that up,
would you?

I have already joined
myself in marriage to
a husband, namely the
kingdom of England.

I'll marry you,
Queenie!

---

43. Elizabeth's father was Henry VIII. Henry married SIX times. He executed two of his
wives, one of whom was Elizabeth's mother, Anne Boleyn. After executing her mother, Henry
married Jane Seymore who died in childbirth. To Elizabeth, marriage meant death.

I'd heard whispers about something called 'the Casket Letters'. I mentioned it in passing to Sam and he explained that they are love poems written between Lord Bothwell and Mary before Mary's second husband, Lord Darnley, was murdered. The letters were used to prove that Mary knew Lord Bothwell was going to murder Darnley and to justify them removing Mary from the throne of Scotland. It is rumoured Queen Elizabeth keeps copies hidden away, but hardly anyone has actually seen them. Some people even think the letters are forgeries. I guess we aren't the only ones secretly writing letters. I wonder what people would make of our letters if they found them long after we are gone...

I'm sorry your sewing lessons aren't going so well. It is **A BIT TRICKY** at first. At least you know how to get rid of bloodstains! If you don't improve, perhaps our business could be a dressmakers and laundry. I wouldn't want you to lose any fingers! We could call it **LACE AND LYE**? What do you think? I would make the dresses and you could take in fine linens and wash them. I had no idea laundry was so complicated! Mary is lucky to have you to keep her smelling sweet.

Your friend,
Kat

12th November 1585
Tutbury Castle, Staffordshire

Dear Kat,

I love the idea of **LACE AND LYE**! Wouldn't it be wonderful? I would like to have my own business one day. My father says he would like to set up a brewery, but we don't have enough money. It's a shame; I think he would be good at it. He has learned a lot since he has moved here. It's hard work, but I like that it keeps him in one place though.

When he was a post rider, galloping off with letters and documents here and there, I missed him. Especially when I was in London without Mother. The road can be dangerous and I was always worried that one day he would not come back. It comes in handy now and then though, eh? It would have been much harder staying in touch without him and his friends ferrying our letters up and down the country. There would be no way we would have had the money!

We haven't got long until Christmas now. I am looking forward to having a holiday! It is getting colder and colder here at Tutbury. It is so cold and draughty! I am sure it is warm at court. Are there lots of parties around Christmas? I am sure it must be your father's busiest time of year! I wish I could see it.

Your friend,
Nell

12th December 1585
Court of Queen Elizabeth, London

Dear Nell,

Court is **SUCH A WONDERFUL PLACE** at Christmas. The queen loves Christmas. December can be a little dull as there is fasting and lots of going to church and saying prayers, but on the 25th there is a marvellous feast. The palace looks like a magical land from a fairy tale decorated with garlands of holly and bay leaves strung together with ivy. It **SMELLS DELICIOUS** too. The **MOUTH-WATERING** scent of spices and fruits from the minced pies drifts from the palace kitchens and fills the halls.

It is my father's busiest time of year, and his favourite. He says the smells remind him of his childhood and the rich spices his mother used in their foods all year round and the oranges he and his friends would pick from trees that lined the streets. Can you imagine orange trees on the streets of London? No one would ever go hungry again!

This year my father has a special honour. He will play the trumpet as the boar's head is brought in. The boar's head is such a special dish that it has its own song and fanfare. I think it looks rather gross, but members of the court get incredibly excited. I don't think I could **EVER** bring myself to eat it.

As well as boar's head, there are all types of other roast meats. Peacocks and swans are served, decorated with their feathers. I think it makes them look as though they are still alive – it's **TERRIFYING**.

But Queen Elizabeth does not actually dine on this rich

and delicious food. She has her meals by herself. The food is a display of **HER WEALTH** and **POWER**. What is not eaten by members of the court is passed out to her staff, and what is left after that is passed out to the poor. After that there are **ELEVEN MORE DAYS** of partying and feasting, with plays and acrobats and even more delicious foods.

The queen gives everyone at court a gift at Christmas. For my father, this is usually money which he tries to put towards my apprenticeship. Then, everyone at court is expected to give the queen a gift on 1st January. Queen Elizabeth **LOVES PRESENTS**.

As people of the court present Her Majesty with gifts, one of the queen's secretaries notes down who gave what. The gifts the courtiers give the queen are expected to be of greater value than the ones she has given them. This is to show **HOW MUCH** they love her. She gets all kinds of things; gowns, fans, looking glasses, even gloves filled with coins.

I don't think it is fair to expect bigger gifts than the ones you give when you are a queen who has **EVERYTHING**. This year my father is giving her a song — one he has worked hard on and wrote **JUST** for her. He is going to perform it for the queen at the ceremony. I hope she likes it!

My favourite part of Christmas, even more than the feasts and the dancing, is the **BANQUET OF SWEETS**. They make all sorts of things out of sugar, from animals to fruits and even games. Some of the sweets are covered with gold and some have spices in them. Last year, Father brought me some sweets and **AN ORANGE**[44] after the party. I wish oranges did grow on trees in London. They really are delicious!

Wishing you and your mother a very merry — and not too cold — Christmas!

Lots of love,
Kat

---

44. Oranges can only be grown in conservatories in England. In Elizabethan times they were considered very exotic and only the very wealthy would have seen one, let alone eaten one.

Dear Kat,

Christmas sounds wonderful at court. I think I would like the **BANQUET OF SWEETS! YUM!** Did your father bring you another orange? I wish you could send me some; they sound delicious.

Needless to say, there wasn't a party here. Far from it. As the queen is Catholic, she fasts over Advent from the 1st to the 24th of December, and eats no meat or milk or cheese, and much of the household does the same. Not that we laundresses see much in the way of meat, anyway. Instead we had the pleasure of moving house once again. Happy New Year and Happy New Home to us!

I won't miss Tutbury one bit, though Mother says we could well move back there, one day. We are now at Chartley which is much nicer. It certainly isn't as smelly and even though it is winter, the place isn't as cold because there are far fewer draughts. In Tutbury, I never felt like I could get warm whenever I had to go to the castle and the cottage we stayed in wasn't much better.

We live in the main house here. Chartley has a lake around it called a moat and Paulet has made it crystal clear that he expects us to do the laundry there. Mother says he doesn't trust all our coming and going. He doesn't want even so much as a slip of paper getting out. I think he suspects that one or more of us are sneaking messages in our baskets of laundry or under our smocks.

I'm not sure how I am going to get this letter to you. My sewing is better now, so I had been stitching my last letters into the seam of my smock, but now we can rarely leave, that won't do at all.

I refuse to surrender to Paulet. I **WILL** find a way to get my letters to you. I am sure I won't be the only person looking. I will keep my eyes peeled.

Yours,
Nell

P.S. I think I found a way. Fingers crossed this gets to you! Please send your reply to 'The Brewer of Burton', they'll know what to do.

Dear Nell,

Hah! Well, you showed Paulet. Your letter was more than a slip of paper and it made it to me just fine. How did you do it? I promise I won't tell Sam. I'm actually quite good at keeping secrets. Certainly better than he is. I think you are wasted in the laundry, you should be working for Walsingham! When I heard that Mary was being moved to a more secure location, I was worried I wouldn't hear from you.

Things have been very dramatic here over the last few weeks. The queen is **FURIOUS** with Sir Robert Dudley, Earl of Leicester and everyone is walking on eggshells around her. The Earl of Leicester was sent to the Netherlands to help the Dutch Protestants in their fight against the Spanish.[45] Elizabeth helped the Dutch to win, and they asked her to be their queen. Elizabeth refused, not wanting to anger the Spanish any more than she had already.

As she had refused they instead asked Leicester to be their Supreme Governor and he accepted. Elizabeth could not believe it, her own advisor accepting a position as a supreme ruler of another nation.

---

45. In the 1500s, Dutch Protestants wanted to be independent from Spain who insisted that everyone who lived in the Netherlands accepted the Catholic faith or suffer torture and execution.

There's a rumour that Leicester's wife, Lettice, will travel out there to join him with a host of ladies to make her own court, just like Her Majesty's.[46] This must have driven Elizabeth crazy.

My father said Elizabeth was **IN LOVE** with Leicester, and that they were sweethearts **FOR YEARS**. But there is little sign of that at the moment. Mary, Queen of Scots, had best not put a foot wrong now. Elizabeth looks ready to **MURDER** just about anyone! I hope she gets some better news soon or we'll all be for it.

Yours,
Kat

46. Elizabeth and the Earl of Leicester, Sir Robert Dudley, had known each other since they were children and were imprisoned in the Tower of London at the same time. They were sweethearts for many years, until Sir Robert married. They remained close but Elizabeth did not warm to his wife.

Dear Kat,

I'm sorry Queen Elizabeth is so angry. I hope she calms down soon! Why doesn't she want to be queen of the Netherlands? I thought kings and queens wanted to be kings and queens of as many places as possible.[47] Isn't that why they send ships all over the world? To try to find new lands? The Netherlands is right on her doorstep!

It's strange, your queen is in **DESPAIR** when mine is in **HIGH SPIRITS**. Mary had been in a sad way for some time. Her rheumatism has been awful. We were washing so many bandages and handkerchiefs, I was wondering how long she could go on like this, but then something seems to have cheered her up. Instead of lying in bed and only seeing her ladies and physician, Mary now spends much of the day squirrelled away with her secretaries. What they are doing is anybody's guess, but it seems they are writing letters. Mary's letters are supposed to be read by Paulet before she sends them, but I know that some of them are not. I know this because I think **I HELPED SEND ONE!**

I will tell you how it happened, but you mustn't tell **ANYONE** - not even Sam! I had finished spreading out the laundry to dry, and was hurrying to meet Agnes to do some sewing when I was stopped by one of Mary's secretaries. He was talking to Paulet while holding a shirt and looking **VERY ANNOYED**.

---

47. At one point, Mary, Queen of Scots, believed she was the rightful queen not only of Scotland but of France and England, too.

**Secretary:** 'Laundry girl! Take this to the cellar and make sure it is cleaned thoroughly.'

**Paulet:** 'The cellar? The laundresses use the moat for the laundry.'

**Secretary:** 'Do I look like a laundress? I don't care what they do with the shirts. I just need this one cleaned. Here! Don't just stand there staring. Take it!'

I scurried over and took the shirt. As Paulet strode off, the secretary bent to whisper, 'Remove the bung from the last barrel of beer and put this in.'[48] He pressed a narrow wooden box into my hand 'Make sure no one sees, eh?'

I took the box and headed down to the cellar as quickly as I could, with it hidden away from sight under the shirt. I really hoped Paulet didn't return all of a sudden. I don't like being near him when I don't have to, never mind when I am carrying a **SECRET PACKAGE**.

When I got to the cellar, I **OPENED** the box. I know I shouldn't have, but I couldn't resist. I wish I hadn't bothered though. At first I thought it was a letter, but when I tried to read it, it was nonsense! This is what it said:

$$n \mathcal{f} c / \text{\#} \quad \alpha c \mathcal{f} \mathcal{f} \quad \sim c \quad \sim \mathcal{3} s c$$
$$/ \sqcap \mathcal{3} - \alpha \quad \varrho \mathcal{3} - s \quad n \mathcal{f} \mathcal{3} \alpha$$

You see! Perhaps it's a different language, though not one I've ever come across. I closed up the box and put it in the barrel. I hope that is what the secretary meant for me to do. Then I went upstairs and

---

48. Mary, Queen of Scots, used lots of different methods for getting her letters out, one of which was in the barrels of beer delivered to Chartley.

asked the kitchen for a sheep's bladder. I put in your letter and sewed it shut before running down to the cellar and pushing it into the barrel. Someone from the brewery picks up empty barrels once a week when they deliver new ones. I'm not sure what they make of what they find in there.

I asked Father to look out for it, and see if he could get it to one of his old post riders. He wasn't pleased when I told him what I had done. He said it was dangerous and that it could have lost him his job at the brewery. He said there have been people coming to the brewery and speaking to the owner about the barrels. He said at first he couldn't find the bladder. He thought I had been telling stories. But then he saw the owner walk out carrying it. He said the owner looked very embarrassed. Father rescued it, thank goodness! What if the owner had looked inside?

I made him swear not to tell Mother. I don't think I could bear having to be the one to tread the lye again!

Yours stealthily,
Nell

18th June 1586
Court of Queen Elizabeth, London

Dear Nell,

My goodness! A sheep's bladder? No wonder my letter was a
**BIT SMELLY** when it arrived. It was dry though, so well done!
Be careful, won't you, Nell? I would hate our letters to get
you into any trouble. Or for your father to lose his job. I don't
think our letters would cause anyone harm, but passing letters
for the secretary is something else! I promise I won't tell Sam.
He hasn't been around as much of late as he has been so
busy with Walsingham – they seem to working on something
very important.

The queen doesn't want to be queen of the Netherlands
because becoming it would mean almost certain war with
Spain! She has already angered them quite a bit by supporting
the Dutch, and she is trying not to anger them any further.

The Netherlands is made up a group of independent
provinces that want to be free to worship as they choose and
govern themselves, and instead they are ruled by the Spanish.
The previous king of Spain, Charles V, had imposed Catholicism
on the people of the Netherlands and demanded everyone
attend Catholic mass. He made a law that meant people could
be killed for attending Protestant services. Thankfully for the
people in the Netherlands he didn't really enforce that law and
people continued to worship as they wished.

Philip was not so lax. He insisted on enforcing the law with
violence and terror and the people rebelled, wanting to push

out the Spanish once and for all. Elizabeth has been helping the Dutch by sending money to support the fighters. This has made Spain angry and they were angrier still when Elizabeth paid for this help with gold plundered from Spanish ships by her privateers.[49] Elizabeth, of course, denied all knowledge, but everyone knows these pirates work for her.

The Spanish would like nothing more than to get rid of Queen Elizabeth and put Mary on the throne. The former Spanish ambassador, a man named Mendoza, was caught plotting as much before he was expelled from the country.[50] But Sam says the Spanish haven't given up. He thinks Mary would be eager to join with them too. She is desperate now her son has refused to share his throne with her; it's only a matter of time before they catch her red handed. He thinks she has promised that if the Spanish free her and put her on the English throne, she will pass succession on to their king when she dies.[51]

Sam is working with a man named Thomas Phelippes who he says is Walsingham's best code cracker. We have been sending little notes to one another in cipher to help us both improve. They're nothing important – usually just arranging when and where to meet. But my point is, I think the letter

49. Privateers were like 'pirates for hire'. They were paid by Queen Elizabeth and others to attack ships and steal the cargo on board. England's most infamous privateer was named Sir Francis Drake.

50. This was during the previous plot headed by an English Catholic nobleman named Francis Throckmorton who passed letters between Mary, Queen of Scots, and the king of Spain through Spanish ambassador, Mendoza. Throckmorton was caught and executed, and the ambassador was expelled from the country.

51. After her son James refused to share the Scottish throne with her, Mary, Queen of Scots, promised to pass succession on to the King Phillip II of Spain after she died if he in turn helped her to defeat Elizabeth and put her on the throne.

you saw was **WRITTEN IN CODE**, I had a quick go at it and I think it says:

'Please tell me more about your plot.'

You see how the writer has substituted each letter for a symbol. They do this so that people can't read what is written; they either think it is nonsense, like you did, or struggle to work out what it means. This would work well, if Walsingham didn't have Thomas Phelippes working with them. Sam says they have already worked out this cipher and know exactly what Mary is sending and to who.

I didn't tell Sam about the beer barrel or about the letter from the secretary. I don't like keeping secrets from him, but I would never do anything that would get you into trouble. I did tell Sam that I was sad that we wouldn't be able to write to one another any more since you had moved to Chartley and he said he might be able to help. He said Walsingham had asked him to go to Chartley to check on Mary's security. He said he will find you when he is there, and he will bring your letter back! I made him swear he would not open them, and I know we can trust him.

Yours,
Kat

Dear Kat,

I think that plan sounds wonderful. Not only will we be able to write to one another without worrying about getting caught, but I will get to meet Sam too! Thank you for letting me know about the cipher. I did not think that the letter from the secretary could be something so underhand. Do you think he could have been writing to the **REAL-LIFE PLOTTERS**? I wonder if they know that Walsingham has such a close watch on them. I hope Mary isn't up to anything. I would hate her to put either Queen Elizabeth or herself in danger!

I have decided I must be more careful. I have made a point of avoiding the secretaries as much as possible and have concentrated on helping Mother with the laundry. She can see I've been working hard and said I might make a good washerwoman yet! When I am not busy doing that, I sew with Agnes (and Hamish of course). I am getting MUCH better.

I felt terrible about putting Father's job at the brewery in danger. He likes working there. He doesn't want to go back to post riding. I hated never knowing when he would have to gallop off in the middle of the night or how long he would be away. He likes staying in one place and living near my mother and me. He said he hopes that one day we would all be able to live together in the same little house. I think that sounds lovely, but I don't know how we would ever afford it. My father doesn't make much money, and Mother and I don't make much scrubbing linens. Father would like to be a brewer himself. I think he'd be a good one too. He has learned so much, so quickly and the owner is pleased with him, but there is no way that will happen. Mother always says we should count our blessings, and I do, but I would so love to live with Father and all of us not to have to work quite so hard. Perhaps one day, eh?

I will hang on to this letter until I see Sam. I am so glad I will finally meet him!


Your friend,
Nell

18th July 1586
Court of Queen Elizabeth, London

Dear Nell,

I'm so glad the plan worked. Sam was the reason we met in the first place, so it seems right that he is helping to keep us together, now. The seal on the letter was unbroken, so I know he didn't read it. I knew he wouldn't though; he may be a terrible spy, but he is a very good friend.

I am glad you are being careful! Walsingham's spies are **EVERYWHERE** and are watching **EVERYTHING** Mary does. Sam said the security at Chartley is water-tight, he said actually it was **BEER TIGHT**. I froze when I heard him say that. I was worried he knew about your sheep's bladder! He doesn't. **PHEW**! I think he meant that Walsingham knows about the **BREWER OF BURTON** passing messages. Walsingham's spies are intercepting the **SECRET LETTERS** so that they can **MAKE COPIES** of them.

They copy **EVERYTHING** she sends and **EVERYTHING** that is sent to her. They copy them so that they can **DECODE THE CIPHER**. That means they were **VERY CLOSE** to finding the one you sent me. He said that one of the spies found a sheep's bladder not long ago! He warned me look out for anything **ODD** in my beer as who knows what brewers like to flavour their ales with nowadays!

They definitely found the secretary's box in that barrel though and I think it must be **VERY IMPORTANT**. He told me not to tell anyone – he really is the most terrible spy – but he thinks they are very close to **CATCHING MARY** in the act of **PLOTTING AGAINST ELIZABETH**. He says he was there when it was discovered.

Thomas Phelippes was working on a new letter copied from one recently sent by Mary. It was written in cipher, similar to the one you saw. He says he didn't quite catch what was in it, but he said Thomas was pleased with himself and drew gallows[52] on it. He took the letter straight to Walsingham who looked happier than he had ever seen him. I can't imagine Walsingham happy – it gives me the creeps to think of it. I would imagine it would be a bit like Paulet having a singsong. It would take something **HIDEOUS** to put a smile on faces as **MISERABLE** as theirs, don't you think?

---

52. A wooden structure used to hang criminals.

Sam said it had been a **TRAP**. They were just waiting for her to **PUT THE PLOT IN WRITING**, and now she has.

I said I didn't believe anyone could be that clever to come up with such a plan of intercepting the letters. Sam said it wasn't just because Walsingham was clever, but because the plotters weren't the best at keeping secrets (he's one to talk!).

Sam said he would prove it. He said that the conspirators were meeting tonight and he knew where and when. I asked if he would take me with him and show me, and he said he would! My **FIRST** and probably **ONLY SPY MISSION**!

I don't believe it will actually come to anything, but if Sam comes through, I promise I will tell you everything.


Yours,
Kat

Dear Nell,

Sam was right. He sent me a note written in cipher for me to meet him on the steps outside the palace after dark.

$$\sim c\ c\ \alpha \quad \sim c \quad z_3 3 \quad \alpha\ \infty\ c$$
$$+\ \alpha\ c\ n + \quad /\alpha \quad +\ -3 + c\ \alpha$$

### 'MEET ME ON THE STEPS AT SUNSET.'

I snuck out after prayers and found Sam where he said he'd be. He looked **RIDICULOUS** with his cap pulled down and his collar up, but he told me I should do the same so as not to **DRAW ATTENTION** to myself. I tried to reason that we were more likely to draw attention to ourselves running around after dark with our hats over our eyes, but he insisted. We ran down along the bank of the Thames until we came to a tavern.

It was **LOUD AND THE LIGHTING WAS DIM**. We managed to push through the drinkers to an empty room at the back. We **CREPT** inside and hid behind a pile of wooden boxes. Inside the room was a stand covering something with a cloth. Sam told me to stay quiet. He said there was to be a meeting in here that would explain everything, but it could be very **DANGEROUS** if we got caught. No sooner had he said that than the door opened and a group of men walked in.

I crouched down so they couldn't see me. Someone called the man who talked the loudest 'Babington'. Babington said he had something to show the group. He **PULLED THE CLOTH OFF** the stand to reveal a painting of all the men who had just walked into the room. 'One day a painting similar to this will hang in every great household in England. We will be heroes!' Pulling the cloth must have loosened some dust, because at that moment Sam let out **A SNEEZE SO BIG** that he **TRIPPED** over his feet and **FELL HEAD FIRST** from behind the boxes.

Sorry, fellows, didn't mean to interrupt your conspira ... party. As you were, chaps.

A man **SEIZED** him by the ear, and held a **DAGGER TO HIS THROAT** and cried, 'A spy! Listening to our plans! What should I do with him, Babington? Shall I run him through?' I held my breath and crouched lower. I was so frightened until Babington said, 'No. Take him to the street. He's just a boy.'

I watched, **FROZEN** to the spot, as Sam was **DRAGGED** away. I didn't know what to do, so I didn't move and stayed **VERY QUIET**.

With Sam gone the men looked more closely at the painting.

Hey, Babington! I was hoping I'd look a bit more heroic.

The painter is an artist not a miracle worker.

One complained that the painting didn't do him justice. He said that, seeing as this painting showed the heroes that were going to rid England of its heretic queen, he was hoping he'd look a bit more handsome.

When the laughter died down, Babington went on to outline the plan. He said he had written to Mary to get her to agree to it, but they needed to move fast. He said some of them would go to the palace to **KILL ELIZABETH**, while others rode to Chartley to rescue Mary. He said once the **REBELLION** was at full swing, **TROOPS** sailing on **SPANISH SHIPS** sent by King Philip II would land on the South Coast and a Catholic **INVASION** would begin.

The conspirators all cheered and clinked their tankards together. I couldn't believe what I was hearing. Sam was right, there really was a plot to **KILL QUEEN ELIZABETH AND FREE MARY, QUEEN OF SCOTS**, and I was hiding in a room from a crowd of **WOULD-BE ASSASSINS**.

I didn't dare move. I stayed where I was until long after the meeting was over and the men had left. I didn't want to risk someone seeing me. When I was sure the coast was clear, I crept from behind the boxes, pushed my way through the tavern and dashed out into the street. Sam was waiting around the corner.

'Thank goodness you're all right!' Sam said.

'Thank goodness I'm all right?! I wasn't the one dragged from a tavern by a bunch of assassins. You're lucky to still be alive.'

'I was right, wasn't I? Not such a bad spy after all, am I?'

'Can we go over the spilling ale all over the people you were supposed to be hiding from and getting **CAUGHT?**'

Before he could answer, we heard a noise. We ran **ALL THE WAY BACK** to the palace.

Once there, he explained that Babington's conspirators were some of the **WORST SECRET KEEPERS** in London and that everyone knew what they were up to – which was why

Walsingham had used them to trap Mary. The plan really was rather clever, and I was impressed that he had managed to work out exactly where to find the conspirators.

I do feel sorry for Mary to have her fate tied to such a group of vain boasting men. The sooner they are arrested the better for everyone, though I am trying not to think what it will mean for Mary. I'm going to stop writing now, as I am **SO TIRED** from running around the city tonight.

I will send this with my other letter up with Sam. I wonder what will happen next. Do you think Walsingham's men will come for Mary? There can be no doubt that she is involved now. I am so sorry.

Yours,
Kat

12th August 1586
Chartley Castle, Staffordshire

Dear Kat,

Sam brought me your letters. Thank you. I read them and hoped to goodness that there was some other explanation for what you saw, but after what I have witnessed here I know it must be true, because Mary has been **ARRESTED**.

Yesterday, I watched as Mary rode out to go hunting. Paulet went with her and she was surrounded by her usual guard. As she was riding I could see **MYSTERIOUS** riders in the distance. Paulet hung back as Mary rode towards them and I thought for a moment that perhaps she was going to be rescued. Alas, it wasn't a rescue, **IT WAS AN AMBUSH**. The mysterious riders were agents sent by Queen Elizabeth and Walsingham to **ARREST** her. Mary climbed down from her horse and sat on the ground, refusing to move, her shoulders slumped. When she did move, she knelt in prayer as Paulet and the queen's agents waited for her to finish.

When she was done, she climbed back on her horse and followed the agents away from Chartley. I've heard whispers that she has been taken to a nearby house at Tixall.

As I write, there are men searching her rooms. Going through all of her belongings, her papers and her books. I caught a glimpse of some of them and they were covered in the symbols and shapes of the ciphers you mentioned. I knew the queen was sending messages, but I did not know to whom. They arrested her secretaries, too. The men even **SEARCHED HER LAUNDRY**! I don't know who will tidy the mess.

I hope Queen Elizabeth can find it in her heart to show mercy to her cousin. Mary's ladies-in-waiting spend their days **WEEPING** and her pets, particularly Hamish, are restless for her to return. The rest of Mary's servants have been dismissed and will be replaced by people chosen by Paulet. I thought we would have to leave too, but Mother says **WE AREN'T IMPORTANT ENOUGH**. I was sad to say goodbye to Agnes. She made me promise to look after Hamish. Poor pup; no mistress and no Agnes, either.

I hope Mary is allowed to return soon. I wonder what will happen to her. I wonder what will happen to us.

Yours,
Nell

18th August 1586
Court of Queen Elizabeth, London

Dear Nell,

Thank you for your letter. I was wondering whether Mary would be arrested. Babington and the plotters were **ARRESTED**, too. Babington was found hiding among the bushes in St Johns Wood with his face blackened with walnut rind. It seems he had used it to hide in the dark.

No sooner was he arrested than his house was searched, where they found papers predicting the **DEATH** of Queen Elizabeth and all manner of dangerous Catholic documents. I'm not sure what makes a document 'dangerous', but Sam said it with such menace.

After his arrest, Babington **CONFESSED TO EVERYTHING** in the hope that he would receive a pardon. He gave up the names of **ALL** of his conspirators and told the interrogators that Mary was **FULLY AWARE** of all of their plans and had given her support.

When news of his and Mary's arrests spread, it sounded like **EVERY CHURCH BELL** in London was ringing. People were so thankful that the plotters had been caught and their beloved Queen Elizabeth remains safe, that some even **HELD PARTIES** in the street and lit huge bonfires.

As this was happening all I could think about was you and Hamish, and everyone else in Mary's court. Of course, I am happy that Queen Elizabeth is safe, but it can mean only **ONE THING** for Mary, Queen of Scots. Sam says the Bond of Association is clear on what is to happen next. He said Elizabeth has given Mary enough chances,[55] and while she may not wish to order the death of an anointed queen,[56] she no longer has a choice. I asked what he meant by an ‹**ANOINTED QUEEN**› and he said that being a king or queen isn't like a normal job, like being a spy or a musician or a laundress, but a holy office – this means that only God has the right to kill them.

Elizabeth doesn't want to kill Mary, because she believes that as Mary is a Queen of Scotland she would be going against God, even though Mary was prepared to **KILL HER**.

55. The Babington Plot was one of a number of plots against Elizabeth but was the first in which Mary was caught in the act of being part of the conspiracy.

56. Elizabeth and many other people believed that kings and queens were given their right to rule by their Christian god. They believed that to kill a monarch would be against their god and that after they died they would be punished for eternity.

Sam said if Elizabeth does order Mary's death, it could be used in the future as an example to others that the killing of kings and queens isn't a crime against God.

Nell, do you know what you and your family will do if the worst happens?

Yours,
Kat

30th August 1856
Chartley Castle, Staffordshire

Dear Kat,

I am glad the **HORRIBLE PLOTTERS** have been arrested. I would hate for Mary to suffer the consequences of this plot alone. I am not sure what Mother and I will do. She said Father still had work with the brewery but that it wasn't enough to support all of us. She didn't seem to be too worried though. She said she couldn't imagine someone like Paulet reading the lye to get his shirts looking fresh.

Until they invent a magical machine for doing all this, there will always be work for laundresses.

She might have said this to **STOP ME** from worrying, but I am sure we will find something. I am more worried about Mary and Hamish. When Mary was returned to Chartley, she was upset to discover that her rooms had been searched and that Queen Elizabeth's men had taken so many of her treasured belongings. She was so miserable, she took to her bed and hasn't been seen since. As most of her loyal staff had been dismissed in her absence, I think she is finding it even lonelier in the castle.

It **BREAKS MY HEART** to think of street parties and celebrations happening in London, while Mary, Queen of Scots, looks as though she might die of **DESPAIR**. I suppose that would save Queen Elizabeth from having to get her hands **DIRTY** and make good on the bond, but it would be a sad end for Mary.

I am sorry to write with so little happy news.

Yours,
Nell

10th September 1586
Court of Queen Elizabeth, London

Dear Nell,

I was so sorry to receive your letter, though I was not surprised to hear that Mary is so low. Do you think she really might **DIE OF SADNESS**? How awful, though I think that is what Elizabeth wants, or for someone else to murder Mary out of loyalty to her. **ANYTHING** to avoid parliament deciding Mary's fate.[57]

Sam says there will be a trial and that he will get to go to it. I wonder if you will, too. Perhaps you will be able to spend some time together. I would like you to get the chance to know one another. He might even be a comfort to you. I know he wants to meet Hamish. Sam says Mary will **DEFINITELY** be found guilty, but they have to have one anyway or it isn't fair. And if the decision has already been made that Mary is guilty, what is the purpose of the trial? It all sounds like a waste of time to me.

I still wish Elizabeth and Mary could sit and talk to one another. Father says England used to be Catholic, but then it was Protestant and then Catholic again.

---

57. Elizabeth knew that if parliament decided the fate of Mary, there would be nothing to stop them from deciding her fate, or that of the kings and queens who would follow her. She would be putting the lives of kings and queens, who she believes are God's representatives, in the hands of ordinary (if very posh) people.

Despite these differences, everyone here is pretty much the same – we are all worrying about the same things and getting on with our lives.

I don't see what difference it makes, do you?

Yours,
Kat

27th September 1586
Fotheringhay Castle
Northamptonshire

Dear Kat,

Thank you for your letter. I don't see what difference being Catholic or Protestant makes. All I care about is that there is a king or queen who is **GENTLE** and **FAIR**. Many people say Elizabeth is tolerant, but I don't see it.

We've moved again, from Chartley to a place called Fotheringhay Castle. What a journey it was! Queen Mary, who has not left her bed since her arrest, could barely ride. Her legs were **SO SWOLLEN** that she was a pitiful sight.

Once again, everything had to be loaded on to carts, some twenty of them or more, and hauled more than eighty miles over bumpy roads and open country.

All we can do now is wait for the trial. If Babington has confessed and even Mary's secretaries have confirmed that the letter Phelippes deciphered is identical to the one written by Mary, what can be done? I don't think it's fair. Mary may have written those letters, but what choice did she have? She was **TRAPPED**.

I will send this letter with Sam if he comes. Father is back near Chartley and I don't know any of the riders here.

Do write to me soon.

Yours,
Nell

Court of Queen Elizabeth, London

Dear Nell,

Sam brought me your letter. He will be coming back up to Fotheringhay tomorrow with Walsingham and Cecil. So you will see him again **SOON**. I will get this to him before he goes. This time Sam will be staying for the **WHOLE TRIAL**. I'm sure he will tell you **EVERYTHING** that is going on. He is a lovely fellow, but he is **TERRIBLE** at keeping secrets.

I supposed that must mean the trial will begin soon. I wonder how long it will last, and what will be decided. I agree that there is little else the trial can conclude other than **MARY'S GUILT**.

   I do hope it won't be too horrible.

   Hug Hamish for me, won't you?


Yours,
Kat

Dear Kat,

Sam has arrived! He came and found me not long after the queen's representatives arrived. He promised to **TELL ME EVERYTHING** that is going on, just like you said. He even said he would **SNEAK ME** into the trial if he could. So yes, Sam is a **SHOCKINGLY BAD SPY**. But, he hasn't been caught yet, so maybe he has been a **TERRIFIC SPY** this entire time? Either way, I am ever so glad he is here.

Walsingham and Cecil have arrived too. You were certainly right about them. They are as grumpy looking as Paulet. You'd think they might look **A BIT** cheerful. This is clearly what all three of them have spent the last twenty years hoping for, but no. **STERN NODS** and **GLOOMY LOOKS** are the order of the day. Even Mother commented on it, she said they ought to tread the lye for a week. That would give them something to look miserable about, I can tell you. You were right to describe Walsingham as looming about, too. To think Sam had him mistaken for your father! I would much rather assist a court musician like your father than Walsingham with all of his sneaking around.

While I knew what they would all be like from your letters, Sam said Mary wasn't the monster he had imagined her to be. She looked so old and sickly that he **ALMOST FELT SORRY FOR HER**.

I would hug Hamish for you, but I haven't seen much of him since the queen returned after her arrest. He refuses to leave her side. I miss him, but I know she needs him more than I do right now.

Sam says riders are taking letters between the trial and Elizabeth's court every day, so he will make sure this goes with it. He may be a terrible spy, but I think he is a **VERY GOOD FRIEND**.

I promise I will write soon.

Love,
Nell

13th October 1586
Court of Elizabeth I

Dear Nell,

I got your letter! I was worried I wouldn't hear from you until Sam got back. He is a wonderful friend. Funny you should say that Sam makes a terrible spy, though. I was thinking how you would make an **EXCELLENT** one. You have managed to get your letters past all of the queen's agents in England!

Even Mary's secretaries with all of their experience and training were caught in Walsingham's trap.

I am glad you and Sam are together, but I will admit that I feel a bit **LEFT OUT** with both of you up there. Do tell me what is happening when you can. I hope it isn't too distressing for you or indeed anyone else.

I will send this up with another rider. News arrives every day, so you should get it soon.

Yours,
Kat

15th October 1586
Fotheringhay Castle
Northamptonshire

Dear Kat,

Goodness, I don't think I would like being a spy at all. There's **TOO MUCH** secrecy! All of this plotting and pretending. Though I suppose I did enjoy going behind Paulet's back and breaking his rules, but that was to write to you!

The trial was held on the second floor of the castle in a large room. Sam was good on his promise and took me in to see it. At one end of the room I noticed, a red velvet chair beneath a white linen Cloth of State. I asked Sam if that chair was for Mary, and he said it was actually for Queen Elizabeth.[58]

The sides of the room were lined with benches for councillors from Elizabeth's court. It looked very formal, but I think you were right. It is a waste of time. Everyone here made their mind up about Mary long before this trial or even before any plot. I don't think she stands a chance.

When the session began, **MARY DID NOT APPEAR!** She sent word that she refused to recognize the court's authority and would not answer **ANY** of their questions. She believes that because, as she is a queen, this court of commoners has no right to judge her and so she does not have to answer to them. She also said that as a queen of Scotland, she is exempt from the laws of England, so cannot be tried for treason. I wonder if everyone is allowed to plead that defence, or whether it is only for kings and queens.

58. Queen Elizabeth was never meant to attend the trial. The chair was a symbol of her authority over the court and a reminder that it had been called in her name.

Cecil sent people in and out of Mary's chamber, and even went in himself, but Mary would not cooperate and is now demanding a trial in London, in front of **ALL OF PARLIAMENT!**

Sam said Cecil told her that the court will proceed whether she is there or not. This must have changed her mind, because I got word this morning that the queen was going to appear. I snuck in shortly before nine.

I was just in time, for soon after, men began to line the benches along the sides of the court. Once they were seated, Mary entered and the council removed their hats as a mark of respect. She was wearing a beautiful black velvet gown with a veil I recognized, made of fine cotton from France.

It was a bit of a blur after that. Mary was questioned by Cecil and presented with the letters intercepted by Walsingham's men, including the one Sam told you about. When Mary saw it, she claimed to never have seen it, nor ever to have heard of Babington and his men. It was clear she did not know how strong the case against her was, or that her secretaries had **CONFESSED** that, not only was the letter hers, but that they had written and sent it for her at her request.

When all the evidence had been heard and questions had been asked, I was expecting the council to retire and return to tell the court whether they believed Mary to be guilty, but they did not. Instead, they are going to leave! Sam said it was under orders of Queen Elizabeth. I am sure they will find her guilty.

I don't think I will be able to get my letters to you for a while. A new jailor has been assigned to watch Mary during the trial, and if I've learned anything while serving Mary, it's that a new jailor means **EVEN MORE SECURITY**. Sam says this is because now that Mary's end is almost assured her supporters might go to desperate lengths to free her.

I will send this letter to you with Sam who will return to London tomorrow. It was nice having someone to talk to about these things. I really will miss him. I am not sure what will happen now. Sam thinks that it is only a matter of time before Elizabeth calls for Mary's execution. I hope he is wrong.


Yours,
Nell

30 October 1586
Court of Queen Elizabeth, London

Dear Nell,

Sam is back, he brought me your letter and told me about the trial. He said that the evidence was brought back to London and presented before parliament. They found Mary guilty, without her being there. I don't think there was ever any chance of another verdict.

It is sad that in order for Queen Elizabeth and England to be safe from Spanish invasion and religious turmoil, Mary must be treated in this way. But it is also hard to imagine the situation would be different if the roles were reversed. When Elizabeth's Catholic sister, Queen Mary I, was on the throne, it was **ELIZABETH IN JAIL**. Queen Mary believed that Elizabeth was conspiring with rebels to **TAKE HER THRONE** and **OVERTHROW** the Catholic church. And now, Mary, Queen of Scots, has been jailed for the same thing. But she has been found guilty.

It does make me wonder how it will all end. Do you think that one day Protestants and Catholics will be able to live peacefully without plotting against one another?

While I am sure you are glad that Mary lives, I can't help wondering what kind of life it can be. Knowing that your execution could be ordered at any moment. Father said that none of us know when it is time to die, that it is God's decision, but in Mary's case it is Queen Elizabeth's.

Sam says Elizabeth is delaying making the verdict public

because she does not want to sign Mary's death warrant.

I guess we will have to wait. I think Queen Elizabeth is hoping somebody will act under the Bond of Association. The bond clearly states that citizens are authorized to murder anyone found plotting against Queen Elizabeth. I know Mary has a lot of enemies. Do you think anybody would go so far as to murder her?

Yours,
Kat

30th November 1586
Fotheringhay Castle
Northamptonshire

Dear Kat,

It is interesting that you ask whether anyone would murder
Mary. There are plenty who would be able to. She is surrounded
by armed guards, sworn to protect Queen Elizabeth. As to who
might **WANT** to see her dead, I would have to say Paulet. He has
always treated her **HORRIBLY** and his loyalty to Queen Elizabeth
is obvious. He's not been short of chances, either. I wonder why he
has not. Maybe he sees Mary as more of a queen than he lets on.
I will keep an eye on him. Not that I would be able to prevent him
if he took it upon himself.

As to how Mary is doing, things are much as they were before.
She is **KIND TO HER STAFF** and even does her best to comfort
them. Some have lived with Mary, serving her, for most of their
lives and do not know what they will do without her.

I am glad Elizabeth has not signed the warrant. While I know
it is unlikely, I am still hoping Elizabeth will find it in her heart
to take **PITY** on her cousin. I do not know how it will all end,
whether Protestants and Catholics will allow each other to live
their lives in peace, free from spying and suspicion.

Do you think there is any hope that Elizabeth will show
mercy on her cousin? She is well known for her tolerance, surely
now would be the time for her to show it. I can only believe it

will end when someone shows some mercy.

I am not sure how I will get this letter to you. There are fewer riders going between here and London nowadays and security is even tighter in case anyone makes a last ditch attempt to rescue Mary. I promise I will write when I can.

Yours,
Nell

Dear Nell,

I'm sorry it has taken me so long to write. I could not find anyone to take my letters. Queen Elizabeth has signed Mary's death warrant.[59] I am so sorry. Sam said Queen Elizabeth had stalled as long as she could, but I don't think she could hold off any longer because there are rumours that **SPANISH SHIPS** have landed on the coast of Wales. Some are saying Catholics, loyal to Mary, are preparing to take up arms against the Crown.[60]

The queen's advisors made it clear that unless Elizabeth wanted to risk **WAR** on English soil, she must sign the warrant and **END THE UNCERTAINTY**. I do not know when this will happen but I wanted to tell you as soon as I heard.

I have other news too; my father has secured an apprenticeship for me at a draper in Lombard Street.[61] I am so excited, but it means I will have to live in the shop.

I will miss being at court with Father. I will miss Sam, too. I do hope you and I can still write to one another. I will send you my address as soon as I know it, otherwise Father can pass it on. Sam is heading up to Fotheringhay with a letter from Walsingham tonight, so you should get this soon!

Your best friend,
Kat

---

59. After signing Mary's death warrant, Elizabeth asked her council not to send it. She did not want to be responsible for Mary's death. In a secret meeting, the Privy Council agreed to send it to Fotheringhay without telling her.

60. These rumours were unfounded. Some believe they were started by members of the Privy Council to force Elizabeth to sign the warrant.

61. If a stylish Elizabethan needed fine cloth or a new outfit they could head to the many drapers of Lombard Street in London.

5th February 1587
Fotheringhay Castle

Dear Kat,

I got your letter and saw Sam. I was worried he had ridden up here with the warrant but he had not. It was only a letter for Amyas Paulet. He said he didn't know what was in it, but I think I might have some idea.[62]

Not long after Sam had delivered the letter, I passed Paulet's study. As I neared the door, it flew open and Paulet **STORMED** out, muttering loudly to himself and looking **UPSET**. He was red in the face and saying that he would not 'shipwreck his soul.'[63] He was so angry he didn't even see me standing there.

I know I said I would be careful, and I have been. I swear, but seeing Paulet so angry and knowing about the death warrant and the letter Sam had brought, I was **DESPERATE TO KNOW MORE**. I waited until I was sure he wouldn't come back before creeping inside to see what might have caused him to **FLY INTO A FURY**. I hurried to his desk to see if I could find the letter Sam had brought. It was from Walsingham, telling Paulet that the queen wanted him to **MURDER MARY** himself under the Bond of Association. There it was in plain ink, a request for him to serve his beloved Queen Elizabeth and he will not.

I have to say, I am surprised he turned down the opportunity,

62. After signing the death warrant, Elizabeth forbade her council from sending it. She still hoped someone would act on her behalf. She asked Walsingham to send word to Paulet that she would be grateful if he would do the deed.

63. Elizabethans believed that to kill a monarch was one of the worst crimes anyone could commit and that after they died they would be punished in hell for eternity by their god.

and think more highly of him than I had done before. Which wasn't hard because I still think he is the **MOST HORRID MAN I HAVE EVER MET**. I will try and get this letter to Sam to take back with him.

With the warrant signed, any hope I have for Elizabeth to take pity on her cousin has gone. I think it is only **A MATTER OF TIME**. I hope you get this letter. I am so happy to hear your news about the apprenticeship. Sam said you were excited. I am sure it will be a lot of hard work, but I know you will do wonderfully. I only hope wherever we end up is half as exciting.

Yours,
Nell

Dear Kat,

I have not heard from you, but I had to write to tell you. Queen Mary is no more. A few days ago, the Earl of Kent arrived with two men. They spoke with Paulet and he took them to see Mary in her chamber.

The earl read the charges against Mary, Queen of Scots, and told her that **SHE WAS TO BE EXECUTED** the following morning on the orders of Queen Elizabeth. Mary listened in silence. When they were done, she thanked them and assured them she was ready.

That night she gathered her servants together to give them gifts from her possessions. There was much **WEEPING** and she comforted them as best she could.

On the morning of her execution, I wanted to be there to wish her well in her final moments. Knowing a mere laundress would not be welcome, I snuck up to the hall and hid outside the door.

Mary played her part well. If she was frightened she showed no sign of it. With her were two of her ladies and two gentlemen, one of whom she asked to help her mount the scaffold that had been erected in the centre of the room.

She was finely dressed, as always, and **PROTESTED HER INNOCENCE** to the last, claiming she had no knowledge of **ANY PLOT** against Elizabeth.

Once Mary was up on the scaffold, she asked to see her priest, but this was denied. She was offered one of the Protestant faith, but she declined. Then her ladies helped her remove her veil and headdress to ready her for the axe. She attempted to give the small cross she wore around her neck to her lady, but the executioner took it for himself.

When she was ready, she kissed her ladies farewell, before letting one of them tie a handkerchief over her eyes. Then she knelt before the block and placed her neck upon it, praying aloud. The executioner did not like this and interrupted her prayers.

I must have shut my eyes, because when I opened them, the crowd was beginning to depart and a sheet covered what remained of Mary on the platform.

As I looked at the sheet, I almost screamed, because IT MOVED! For a moment I thought it might be **A GHOST**, or some terrible spirit, but my fear turned to pity when I heard a **SAD YELP**. It was **HAMISH**! He must have followed Mary under her skirts!

When the last of the crowd was almost gone, I rushed to rescue Hamish. I **DREAD** to think what the executioner would have done with him, if he had found him. The poor dog was shaking and so was I. He had blood on his paws, so without a second thought I washed them clean, fed him some bread and held him close. The bath seemed to **CHEER HIM UP** quite a bit, which helped to calm my nerves, too.

When we were ready, I returned him to Mary's ladies who were weeping in her rooms. They thanked me and cried even more before paying me two whole pounds. I wanted to say no to the money, that it was the least I could do, but I knew the money could help my family. Two pounds is **MORE MONEY** than we could hope to see in a **LIFETIME** of laundry. It could even help Father set up a brewery!

I asked what would become of Hamish, and they said they didn't know. They didn't know what was going to become of themselves. That is when I said, 'I could look after him'. The ladies agreed to this as the best plan. So although I have lost Mary, I have gained a dog.

I know Mary loved Hamish very much, so I am happy to do this small service to her. To give her beloved dog as happy a life as possible.

I don't know what we will do now. We will go to Burton tomorrow and stay with Father. I wonder what he will make of the money, and of Hamish!

If we return to London, I will come and find you at the draper's. I hope your apprenticeship is **EVERYTHING** you wanted and more. You are a **GREAT FRIEND**.

Until we meet again,
Nell and Hamish

6th July 1603
Handsome Prints
London

Dear Kat,

At least, I hope it is you! I am **BACK IN LONDON**! I was walking down Lombard Street when I spotted a sign saying, Lace and Lye. **I COULDN'T BELIEVE MY EYES**. Is this your shop? Did you really start the business after all? Do you make lovely things? Gosh, how **EXCITING**. I really do hope it is you.

I asked after you but the man didn't want to tell me much. I am guessing it is because I looked too dirty to have a fancy gown made. My hands were all inky from my uncle's print shop. I said I'd come back, but I thought I would scribble down this note, to let you know I'm here.

It's been years, hasn't it? I've often thought about you. I have **so MUCH** to tell you. My father started a brewery. We make some of the **FINEST BEER** in all of England, and no, we don't put sheep's bladders in it. Haha.

After Mary was executed, I gave the money to my father. He couldn't believe his eyes. He had never seen so much in **ALL HIS LIFE**. It was a good thing too; with Mother and I out of work, we would have been in a terrible state. He took the money and bought part of a brewing business from a man who wanted to retire.

It's hard work, but the money he and Mother make is their own and I am **PROUD** of them. I keep a record of all the customers and who owes what. I'm in town to help my uncle print some adverts for us, which is why my hands are **COVERED IN INK**.

   I hope you write back! I hope this is you...

Yours,

Nell Anderson


P.S. Do you still hear from Sam? After everything, I do often wonder if he ever became a **SPYMASTER**...

10th July 1603
Lace and Lye
London

Dear Nell,

My goodness! It's been such a long time. I can't believe I
missed you! It would have been **SO GOOD** to see you. I have
always wondered what happened to you after Mary died.
Lace and Lye is my business! My apprenticeship was hard
work, I had to clean the shop, and do **EVERY LITTLE JOB**
the draper and his family didn't want to do, but I learned
all I needed to know to go out on my own. Little jobs at
first, like ruffs and shirts.

Then the people who bought ruffs and shirts wanted
to know if I could make breeches and doublets and hats,
and brought me all sorts of fine velvet and silks to make
it from. I mainly do men's clothes and I even make clothes
for the **ROYAL MUSICIANS**, but I don't get to make gowns,
which was always our dream. I wasn't sure what to call my
business, but then I remembered our letters and I couldn't
**RESIST** calling it Lace and Lye. I am glad I did. How else
would you have found me?

I am **SO HAPPY** to hear your father became a brewer!
What a wonderful thing to have come from such a tragedy.
It was a fine reward for your **LOYALTY** to your mistress and
to her dog Hamish. You deserved it and every good thing
that has happened to you since.

I was sad that Queen Elizabeth died. She served her

country well. It is hard to believe so much has changed since she came to the throne. England is a different country. It is a **SHAME** that Elizabeth never married or had an heir to pass the throne on to. It is strange to think that the son of the woman she feared so greatly will be king.[64]

I wonder what the new king will be like.

I would love to go to the coronation. To see the king pass through the streets and celebrate a **NEW BEGINNING**.

Do you think you might be able to join me? We could meet at the shop first and go along together. Working for our **TWO QUEENS** divided us for so long, wouldn't it be nice if celebrating the new king brought us back together? I'll bring Sam, too.

Speaking of Sam, I hear from him **A LOT**, actually - because **WE GOT MARRIED**! I wish I could see your face when you read that. He didn't become a spymaster, he decided he didn't like sneaking around as much as he thought he would.

It seems fitting, don't you think? A **UNITED ENGLAND** and Scotland, and the **THREE OF US** reunited too!

I hope you can make it.


All my love,
Kat Grant


64. When Queen Elizabeth I died, the throne passed to Mary, Queen of Scots's only son, King James VI of Scotland was crowned King James I of England on 25 July 1603.

# TRUE OR FALSE?

**False**

Kat and Nell, and their families, didn't really exist, but people like them certainly did. Kat's father is based on the black trumpeter John Blanke, who served as a musician to King Henry VIII. John was believed to have travelled to England as an attendant to Henry's first wife, Catherine of Aragon. John appears in artwork of the period. Little is known about what happened to John, but it is known he was a free man who lived alongside the other musicians at court. John Blanke was one of many black people living and working freely in England and Scotland at this time.

Nell and her mother are based on accounts of the security measures put in place while Mary was in captivity. The methods used by Nell, including treading the lye, are typical of the period.

While many more people could read and write under Elizabeth's reign than they had done at any other period in English history, it is very unlikely that girls like Nell and Kat would have been able to.

**True**

The lives of both Mary, Queen of Scots, and Elizabeth I really were as dramatic as described here. All of the imprisonments, plots, marriages, kidnappings, assassinations, trials, code-cracking, beheadings and even disgusting laundry practices took place as described.

Mary and her conspirators really did communicate by passing coded letters in barrels of beer, loads of laundry and even clothes sent from abroad.

Francis Walsingham really did run an international spy network and employed expert code breakers to detect any threats against Queen Elizabeth I.

Mary, Queen of Scots, really did have a loyal white dog who stayed by her side until the very end.

# Timeline of Elizabethan England

**1509**
> Henry VIII becomes king of England.

**7th September 1533**
> Elizabeth I of England is born to Anne Boleyn, second wife of Henry VIII.

**1533**
> Henry VIII leaves the Catholic Church and appoints himself head of the Protestant, Church of England.

**8th December 1542**
> Mary, Queen of Scots, is born in Linlithgow to James V of Scotland and Mary of Guise.

**14th December 1542**
> Mary's father, James V, dies.

**9th September 1543**
> Mary is crowned queen of Scotland. Her mother, Mary of Guise, rules Scotland until she is old enough.

**13th August 1548**
> Mary arrives in France to be raised in the French court.

**18th March 1554**
> Princess Elizabeth (later Queen Elizabeth I) is

imprisoned in the Tower of London suspected of conspiring against her sister, Queen Mary I.

**24th April 1558**
Mary marries the heir to the French throne.

**17th November 1558**
Princess Elizabeth is crowned queen of England. This is when she became queen on the death of Edward VI, but her coronation was not until 15 January 1559.

**10th July 1559**
Mary becomes queen consort of France when her husband Francis II becomes king.

**11th June 1560**
Mary's mother, Mary of Guise, who had been ruling Scotland in her stead, dies.

**5th December 1560**
Mary's husband, King Francis II, dies.

**19th August 1561**
Mary returns to Scotland to rule as queen.

**29th July 1565**
Mary, Queen of Scots, marries Lord Darnley.

**19th June 1566**
Prince James (later King James VI of Scotland and James I of England) is born to Mary, Queen of Scots, and Lord Darnley.

**10th February 1567**

Lord Darnley is assassinated.

**24th April 1567**

Mary, Queen of Scots, is kidnapped by Lord Bothwell, a man suspected of being involved with the assassination of Lord Darnley.

**15th May 1567**

Mary, Queen of Scots, marries Lord Bothwell.

**17th June 1567**

Mary, Queen of Scots, is imprisoned in Lochleven Castle, Scotland for conspiring to murder Lord Darnley.

**24th July 1567**

Mary, Queen of Scots, is forced to abdicate her throne.

**29th July 1567**

Infant James is crowned king of Scotland to become James VI.

**May 1568**

Mary, Queen of Scots, escapes from Lochleven Castle dressed as a washer woman and flees to England.

**Oct 1568-Jan 1569**

Commission investigates whether Mary was involved in conspiring and murdering Lord Darnley. They do not find her innocent or guilty.

## January 1569-1587

Fearing Mary's claim to the throne and the threat of her supporters, Elizabeth I keeps Mary captive, moving her and her court from house to house and keeping her under close watch.

## Spring 1586

Mary becomes involved in the Babington Plot.

## 11th August 1586

Mary is arrested and her papers seized.

## 11th-15th Oct 1586

The trial of Mary, Queen of Scots, takes place at Fotheringhay Castle.

## 29th October 1586

Mary, Queen of Scots, is found guilty.

## 1st February 1587

Elizabeth I signs a death warrant for Mary.

## 8th February 1587

Mary, Queen of Scots, is executed at Fotheringhay Castle.

# PEOPLE FROM HISTORY

**Queen Elizabeth I**
**7th September 1533-14th March 1603**
**(Queen of England: 1558-1603)**

When Elizabeth came to the throne, England was in turmoil. Her sister Mary, who ruled before her, had attempted to restore England to the Catholic Church and executed so many people, she was nicknamed 'Bloody Mary'. When Mary died without an heir, many believed Elizabeth had no claim to the throne, because her father, King Henry VIII, had declared his marriage to her mother, Anne Boleyn, was invalid, and had her beheaded when Elizabeth just three years old.

Despite this, Elizabeth ruled England for forty-four years and became known as one of its most famous and beloved monarchs, so much so that her reign is called the Golden Age. But she was not popular with everyone. Throughout her reign, there were many plots to overthrow and even to assassinate her, but with the help of her advisors and network of spies, plotters such as Babington and William Parry were caught and severely punished.

Elizabeth never married and had no children. When she died in 1603, the throne passed to

James VI of Scotland, her first cousin twice removed and son of Mary, Queen of Scots.

## Mary, Queen of Scots
## 8th December 1542–8th February 1587
## (Queen of Scotland: 1542–1567, Queen Consort of France 1559–1560)

Mary became queen of Scotland when she was six days old. As she was very young, Scotland was ruled on her behalf by advisors, known as regents, and her mother, Mary of Guise. Despite being queen of Scotland, Mary grew up in France where she had been promised in marriage to the heir to the French throne, Francis. Mary married Francis in 1558 and became queen consort of France in 1559 until her husband died a year later. After Francis died, Mary returned to Scotland to rule as queen.

Mary, Queen of Scots, was not popular in Scotland because she was a Catholic at a time when the wealthiest families in Scotland were Protestant. They feared Mary would try to make Scotland Catholic. Instead, Mary agreed to allow people to worship as they wished as long as she was allowed to do the same.

In 1565, Mary, Queen of Scots, married a man named Henry Stewart (Earl of Darnley) and had a child, James (James VI Scotland/James I England) a year later. Darnley was not a good husband. He was ambitious and jealous and was known to be involved in the violent murder of Mary's secretary, David Rizzio.

Darnley died in an explosion in 1567 and many believed he was murdered. Soon after Darnley died, Mary was kidnapped by a man named James Hepburn, Earl of Bothwell and held captive in Dunbar Castle. Bothwell was suspected of having been involved in Darnley's death, so people were scandalized when Mary agreed to marry him.

Mary's marriage caused the wealthy families in Scotland to rise up against her. They forced her to give up her crown in favour of her son, and imprisoned her in Lochleven Castle.

Mary escaped in 1568 and fled to England, where she hoped her cousin Queen Elizabeth, would help her. But Mary was not popular in England either. For not only was she Catholic, but she also had a claim to the English throne. Mary was the granddaughter of Henry VIII's sister Mary Tudor, and many believed that as Henry had declared his marriage to Elizabeth's mother Anne Boleyn was invalid, Elizabeth's claim to the throne was invalid, too. Fearing that supporters of Mary's claim to the throne would rise up against her, Elizabeth held Mary captive for eighteen years. While imprisoned, it is believed Mary was involved in a number of plots against Elizabeth, the last of which, with Anthony Babington, led to her being found guilty of treason and executed in 1587.

## Sir Francis Walsingham
## 1532-1590

Sir Francis Walsingham was a Protestant from a wealthy family who spent the reign of Mary I in exile in Switzerland. When he returned he joined Elizabeth I's government and worked hard to become her principal secretary and one of her most trusted advisors. Walsingham used some of the people he had met on his travels to build a network of agents loyal to Queen Elizabeth I.

Walsingham used code-breaking and secret agents to uncover plots against Queen Elizabeth and is known for being one of England's first spymasters. Walsingham was known for wearing a lot of black and for looming around. It is said that Queen Elizabeth herself who gave him the nickname 'the Moor.'

**If you enjoyed *My Best Friend and the Royal Rivals*, why not read:**

# My
# Best Friend

## THE EVACUEE

Sally
Morgan

Illustrated by
Gareth
Conway

My
Best Friend
ON THE TITANIC

1912

Sally
Morgan

Illustrated by
Gareth
Conway